MAXIMS

C

MAXIMS

OF

CHESS

by

John W. Collins

David McKay Company, Inc.

New York

THIS BOOK IS
FOR

Professor Louis J. Wolff

A LIFELONG FRIEND
AND
TRUE LOVER OF CHESS,
with whom I have been exchanging
maxims for many years

COPYRIGHT © 1978 BY JOHN W. COLLINS

Library of Congress Cataloging in Publication Data

Collins, John W
  Maxims of chess.

  Includes indices.
  1. Chess—Quotations, maxims, etc. I. Title.
GV1445.C69   794.1   77–18245
ISBN 0–697–50811–2

10 9 8 7 6 5 4 3 2 1

MANUFACTURED IN THE UNITED STATES OF AMERICA

Acknowledgments

My grateful thanks are due to:

Ethel B. Collins, my sister, for reading the manuscript, for corrections, suggestions, and revisions, for checking the proofs, and for numerous helpful tasks.

William J. Lombardy, International Grandmaster, my friend, for interesting McKay in publishing the book, for encouragement, for assisting with the diagrams, for editing, and for expert technical advice.

Mark Levine, my friend and student, for preparing the diagrams, for translations, and for research.

Alan Tucker, manager, general book division, David McKay Company, Inc., for faith in the book, for friendly consultations, and for welcome, professional advice.

JOHN W. COLLINS

Contents

Introduction

Some years ago I bought a copy of *The Elements of Style* by William Strunk, Jr., "with Revisions by E. B. White." This small book of only fifty-one pages, plus "An Approach to Style," a twenty-page final chapter contributed by the reviser, made an immediate and lasting impression. Written in 1918 and privately printed, the book stresses "the principle requirements of plain English style" and became known as "the *little* book" on the Cornell campus, where Strunk was professor of English and White was his friend and student. Professor Strunk was a positive man, with a sense of humor, who took a firm stand for cleanliness, accuracy, and brevity. He would lean forward over his desk, grasp his lapels, and growl at his class: "Rule Thirteen. Omit needless words! Omit needless words! Omit needless words!"

Perhaps it was only natural, therefore, that when I began to search for an idea for my next book in 1976 I thought of a *"little chess book."* But a little book about what? A born kibitzer, I was given to such remarks while playing skittles as "Always check, it may be mate!," "Open files openly arrived at," "My King likes to go for a walk," and "Chess is a hard game." Maxims soon came to mind. Maxims illustrated by examples. I had found my book: *The Little Chess Book.* McKay bought it, and a few months later convinced me the title should be changed to *Maxims of Chess.* Admittedly, the new one is more descriptive, but I have a sense of bereavement. I miss "the little chess book." Still, the concept remains. Brevity and accuracy are still in force. And I can still obey the command: "Omit needless words!"

The book has fifteen chapters. Six on the pieces—King, Queen, Rook, Bishop, Knight, and Pawn—nine on other aspects—The Endgame, The Middlegame, The Opening, Tactical Play, Combinations, Positional Play, Exchanging, Strategy, and A Philosophy of Chess. Each of the first fourteen chapters has an introduction, a maxim, a diagram, an example containing an entire game, part of a game, or an endgame study, all with annotations, and the names, places, and dates connected with the example. The fifteenth chapter is an essay on the game.

The introductions to the chapters on the various pieces describe the value, moves, powers, and underlying characteristics of the particular piece.

The maxims are, I hope, witty and wise. They are taken from the classics, chess literature, famous and not so famous players, and from my own store of quotable quotes (the unattributed maxims are my own). Some have been slightly paraphrased, without damage to their essence. All are linked to the examples beneath them and dramatize a point which is instructive and can be remembered.

The diagrams precede the examples and show the position in the game or study just prior to the move which brings out the main feature of the example. When it was impossible or inconvenient to give the number of the initial move, the device "*White to Move*" or "*Black to Move*" has been employed.

There are 140 games, parts of games, or endgame studies included in the examples. All are annotated, with varying degrees of thoroughness, according to what seemed appropriate. The great majority of the games or fragments were played by world champions, grandmasters, international masters, and masters. Most of the games are of recent vintage, some are old favorites. Every one provides excellent study material. The endgame studies, while few in number, are uniquely suited to illustrate a theme, or the power of a piece, and sometimes even bring out the humorous side of chess.

Naturally, some of the examples are interchangeable: one in the chapter "The King" may fit as well in "The Endgame"; one in "Exchanging" may fit as well in "Positional Play"; one in "Combinations" may fit as well in "Tactical Play"; and so on. But while an example might be equally at home in another chapter, none are misplaced where they appear. The chapter "Exchanging," incidentally, comprises an addition to chess literature. To the writer's knowledge, only Nimzovich and Pachman have contributed specific chapters in their books to this subject, and those are less substantial than the one to be found here.

The initials of players' names have been largely omitted, except when confusion might otherwise result. So too have the names of tournaments. In all but a few cases dates have been verifiable; when not, the error is likely to be slight.

And, finally, the last chapter, "A Philosophy of Chess," is an outline of the origin, development, and spread of chess. The opinions held of it by great men. A tentative attempt to probe its innermost nature. Some thoughts on what and how to develop ability and the mill through which an ambitious player must go. An inquiry into the Fischer Boom. And where do we stand today and what does the future hold?

That is the story of this "little chess book" or *Maxims of Chess*. A book designed to entertain and instruct in a new way. The rest is up to the reader. In concluding the introduction to his revision of *The Elements of Style*, E. B. White writes that if he found himself in the position of facing a class in English usage and style, he would lean far over his desk, clutch his lapels, blink his eyes, and say in pure Strunkian fashion: "Get the *little* book! Get the *little* book! Get the *little* book!" I would rather like to conclude my introduction in a similar way: "Get the *little* book of chess—*Maxims of Chess!*

JOHN W. COLLINS

New York, 1977

The game of chess is the touchstone of the intellect.

GOETHE

The King

The King plays various roles. In the Opening, he is cautious, deliberate, waiting to see whether developments make it wise to castle on the Kingside, the Queenside, or not at all. In the middle-game, he is terrified at the fierce battles which rage across the board and flees to the safest hideout. But in the Endgame he changes character completely and becomes a vigorous, fearless fighter. There powers peculiar to him, and to a lesser extent those of the Queen, make themselves fully felt. As Znosko–Borovsky puts it: **"The King plays a most important part in the end-game, and gains in power and activity as the number of pieces on the board diminishes."** This power and activity must be used. It is a distinguishing feature of grandmaster strategy.

The King is a fighting piece.

—Anonymous

After 23. . . . P–R3

Alekhine–Yates, London 1922.

>   **24. K–B2!**   . . .

The beginning of a mating attack with the King, the two Rooks, and the Knight!

24. . . .	**K–R2**
25. P–R4!	**R–KB1**
26. K–N3	**R/B–QN1**
27. R–B7	**B–N4**
28. R/1–B5!	**B–R3**
29. R/5–B6	**R–K1**
30. K–B4	**K–N1**
31. P–R5!	**B–B8**
32. P–N3	**B–R3**
33. R–B7	**K–R2**

If 33. . . . R–KB1 34. RxRch KxR 35. RxP wins.

34. R/6–B7	**R–KN1**
35. N–Q7!	. . .

Threatening to win the Exchange with 36. N–B6ch and also vacating K5 for the King.

35. . . .	**K–R1**
36. N–B6!	**R/N–KB1**

If 36. . . . PxN 37. R–R7 mate.

>   **37. RxP!**   . . .

An unexpected sacrifice which forces mate in seven moves. Or less

37. . . .	**RxN**
38. K–K5!	**Resigns**

The King administers the coupe de grâce! If 39. . . . QR–KB1 (or 39. . . . KR–B1) 40. R–R7ch K–N1 41. R/B–N7 mate.

The great mobility of the King forms one of the chief characteristics of all Endgame strategy.
—Nimzovich

After 29. . . . R–QB1

Botvinnik–Kann, Sverdlovsky 1943.

30.	**K–N2**	**P–KN4?**
31.	**R–Q5!**	**R–KN1**

If 31. . . . K–K3 32. P–Q7 wins. And if 31. . . . R–B3 32. K–N3 RxP 33. P–K8=Qch wins the Rook.

32.	**K–N3**	**P–B3**
33.	**K–N4**	**K–K3**
34.	**K–R5!**	**. . .**

White's plan is "simple": to win one of the Kingside pawns, sacrifice his QP and KP, and transpose into a won King-and-pawn ending.

34.	**. . .**	**P–R4**

If 34. . . . KxR 35. P–Q7 forces a new Queen. And if 34. . . . R–KR1 35. K–N6 wins.

35.	**KxP**	**K–B2**

Threatening 36. . . . R–R1 mate.

36.	**K–R5**	**R–R1ch**

| 37. K–N4 | R–R5ch |
| 38. K–N3 | . . . |

Not 38. K–B5?? R–B5 mate.

38. . . .	R–R1
39. P–KB4	PxPch
40. KxP	K–K3
41. P–Q7!	. . .

This is the decisive transposition.

41. . . .	KxP
42. P–Q8=Qch	RxQ
43. RxR	KxR
44. K–B5	Resigns

For if 44. . . . K–K2 45. K–N6 (45. P–R4 wins, too) K–K3 46. P–R4 P–B4 47. K–N5! K–K4 48. P–R5 P–B5 49. P–R6 P–B6 50. P–R7 P–B7 51. P–R8=Qch wins.

Watch Tal's King stroll nonchalantly into the heart of the enemy camp.

—Chernev

After 24. . . . RxR

Tal–Lissitsin, Leningrad 1956.

      25. K–Q2!   . . .

The King hits the road.

      25. . . .   **N–N6**
      26. K–B3   **P–B5**
      27. K–Q4   **B–B4**

Trying for 28. . . . BxB 29. KxB R–K6ch 30. K–Q4 R–K7.

      28. R–Q2   **R–K3**
      29. N–B5   **R–R3**
      30. K–K5!   . . .

Tiptoeing through a mine field!

      30. . . .   **BxB**
      31. PxB   **RxP**
      32. K–Q6   **R–R3ch**
      33. K–B7   **N–B4**
      34. K–N7   **N–Q5**

Threatening 35. . . . R–R7 and 36. . . . P–B6.

      35. R–KB2   **P–R4**
      36. RxP   **N–K3**
      37. R–N4ch   **K–B1**

If 37. . . . R–N3 38. RxRch RPxR 39. NxN PxN 40. KxP K–B2 41. P–QN4 PxP 42. PxP K–K2 43. P–N5! K–Q1 44. K–Q6 and White wins.

      38. KxP   **NxNch**

More effective discovered checks are lacking.

      39. KxN   **R–K3**
      40. KxP   **R–QN3**
      41. P–N4   **PxP**
      42. PxP   **K–K2**
      43. K–B5   **R–B3**
      44. R–Q4   **R–B4ch**

45.	K–N6	R–B3ch
46.	K–B7	R–B4
47.	R–K4ch	K–B3
48.	K–B6	R–B7
49.	P–N4	P–R4

If 49. . . . R–Q7 50. P–Q4. If 49. . . . R–QN7 50. P–N5. And if
49. . . . R–B7ch 50. R–B4. So, Black plays for a passed BP.

50.	PxP	K–N4
51.	P–N5	P–B4
52.	R–N4	P–B5
53.	P–N6	P–B6
54.	P–N7	Resigns

For if 54. . . . R–B7ch 55. K–Q5 P–B7 56. P–N8=Q P–B8=Q
57. Q–N3ch K–B3 58. Q–K5ch K–B2 59. R–N7ch and mate in three
moves.

The King is a strong piece. Use it!

—Fine

After White's 32d

Kavalek–Rogoff, Oberlin 1975.

32. . . .	P–B3!!

Endgame tactics! Black's idea is to maneuver the King to the other wing where it can help in the queening of the foremost KBP.

	33. R–K6ch	. . .

If 33. BxP R–B1 34. RxP B–Q5 wins.

33. . . .	K–Q4
34. RxP	K–K5
35. R–B7	R–B2!
36. R–B8	B–B4!
37. R–B6	B–Q5
38. R–B8	B–N2!

The Rook is driven off the KB-file, and the King is enabled to occupy KB6.

39. R–K8ch	K–B6
40. R–K1	B–Q5!
41. P–N4	. . .

A futile attempt at counterplay.

41. . . .	K–N5
42. R–Q1	B–B7
43. R–Q5	R–B2
44. K–B2	P–B5!
45. K–Q1	P–B6
46. P–R4	B–N6!

Now White will be forced to sacrifice his Bishop for the passed pawn.

47. R–Q4ch	K–R6
48. B–K3	P–B7
49. BxP	BxB
50. R–K4	BxP

The reincarnation of the KBP.

51. P–R5	B–B7
52. P–N5	P–R5
53. K–K2	K–N7

54.	P–N6	PxP
55.	PxP	P–R6
56.	R–N4ch	B–N6
	Resigns	

The King dramatically changes roles once in a blue moon and throws caution to the wind in the opening, strides forth to give battle in the middle-game, and reaps the harvest in the endgame, active and powerful from beginning to end.

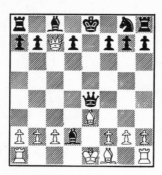

After 9. . . . BxNch

Lombardy–Calvo, Siegen 1970.

10.	KxB	Q–N5ch
11.	Q–B3	QxQch
12.	KxQ	. . .

With the two Bishops and an active King, White already has the upper hand.

12.	. . .	N–K2
13.	B–B5	P–QN3
14.	B–Q6	K–Q1
15.	B–Q3	B–N2

16. KR–K1	N–B1
17. B–R3	B–Q4

If 17. . . . BxP 18. R–KN1 B–Q4 19. RxP.

18. K–Q4!	B–K3
19. P–KB4	P–N3
20. B–K4	R–QN1
21. K–K5	K–B2
22. K–B6	N–Q3
23. BxNch	KxB
24. R–K3	. . .

Threatening 25. R–QB3 and 26. R–Q1ch.

24. . . .	K–B2
25. R–B3ch	K–Q1
26. R–Q1	R–K1
27. B–B3	P–KR4
28. P–QR3	R–QB1
29. RxRch	KxR
30. R–K1	R–Q1
31. B–K4	K–B2
32. R–K3	P–QN4
33. K–K7!	. . .

An active King. Threat: 34. R–B3ch.

33. . . .	R–KR1
34. R–B3ch	K–N3
35. K–Q6	P–R5
36. R–B5	P–R6
37. P–KN3	R–K1
38. B–Q3	P–R3
39. B–K4	B–N5
40. R–K5	R–QB1
41. K–K7	B–K3
42. P–B3	P–Q3
43. R–N5!	R–B2ch
44. K–B6	B–N6

45.	B–Q5	B–B5
46.	P–B5!	PxP
47.	RxP	P–R4
48.	BxB	PxB

And after 49. K–N5 R–K2 50. R–B2 P–B4 51. R–Q2! K–B4 52. KxP White utilized his aggressive King and extra Pawn to force resignation on the 74th move.

An indomitable King and two baleful Bishops are enough to carry most any day.

After 19. . . . K–B1

Matera–Denker, New York 1967.

20.	K–B1	P–N4
21.	B–K1	R–B1
22.	K–K2	N–K1
23.	B–B3	R–B2
24.	R–QB1	P–R3
25.	B–Q3	B–B3
26.	K–Q2	BxN?

Parting with this Bishop brings just plain sorrow on the dark squares.

27. BxB	RxR
28. KxR	N–Q3
29. P–KN4!	K–K2
30. K–B2	P–B3
31. K–B3	N–B2
32. K–N4	B–Q2
33. K–B5	N–Q1
34. K–N6!	. . .

The King just keeps rolling along. Not 34. KxP? B–B3ch 35. K–B5 BxP.

34. . . .	B–B3
35. B–B5ch	K–K1
36. B–N6ch	K–Q2
37. B–B5ch	K–K1
38. K–B7!	. . .

Reaching its destination, the King establishes zugzwang.

38. . . .	P–Q5
39. BxP	BxP
40. B–Q7ch	K–K2
41. B–B5ch	Resigns

My King likes to go for a walk.

—Steinitz

After 32. B–N4

Smirka–Wolff, Brooklyn 1928.

32. . . .	**K–B2!**

This is the first of thirteen steps that lead to QN7! With the pawns interlocked and Bishops of opposite color, this long march is the only way to win the game, despite Black's extra pawn.

33.	P–R4	K–K1
34.	K–Q2	K–Q2
35.	K–K3	B–Q4
36.	K–Q2	K–B3
37.	R–N3	K–N4
38.	K–B1	K–B5
39.	B–B3	B–B3!

Looking ahead to his 44th move.

40.	R–R3	R–N6!

Threatening 41. . . . RxB! 42. PxR KxP 43. R–R2 (if 43. R–N3 K–N6 44. R–R3 KxP wins) 43. . . . P–K6 and mate in three.

41.	B–Q2	KxP
42.	B–K3ch	K–B5
43.	P–R5	B–K1
44.	PxP	BxP

If 44. . . . PxP? 45. R–R8.

45.	R–R1	R–N2

Make way for the King.

46.	R–R3	K–N6
47.	B–Q2	K–R7
48.	B–B3	R–N6
49.	R–K3	. . .

If 49. B–Q4 P–Q7ch wins the Rook.

49. . . .	RxB!

Leaving the rest for the King.

50.	PxR	KxP
51.	R–K1	K–N6
52.	K–Q2	P–R6
53.	R–QR1	K–N7
	Resigns	

The threat to promote the QRP will cost White his Rook.

Castle when you will, or if you must, but not when you can.

—Napier

After 14. . . . P–B3

Seuss–Hurme, Austria 1969.

15. BxB	. . .

This is the beginning of a mating attack.

15. . . .	KxB
16. Q–R8ch	K–B2
17. B–B4ch	B–K3

If 17. . . . N–K3 18. R–R7 mate. And if 17. . . . P–K3 18. N–N5ch PxN 19. R–B1ch K–K2 20. Q–N7 mate.

18. N–N5ch	**PxN**
19. O–O mate!	

Castle when you will. Especially if it mates!

Deny a King his castle and he will sally forth to wreak vengeance.

After 18. Q–B6ch

Ivanovic–Sveshnikov, U.S.S.R. 1976.

18. . . .	**K–K2**
19. BxNP	**R–R2**
20. Q–K8ch	**K–B3**
21. P–KN4	**R–K2**
22. Q–N8	**K–K4!**

Black protects his QP and threatens both the QP and KNP.

23. P–B4ch	**KxBP**
24. K–K2	**. . .**

If 24. QxPch R–K4 25. Q–QB6 Q–Q7 should win.

24. . . .	K–K4
25. KR–KB1	PxP
26. P–N4!	B–N2!

Not 26. . . . QxNP?? 27. R–B5ch! KxR 28. B–Q7ch! RxB 29. QxQ and White wins.

| 27. PxQ | . . . |

If 27. QxR QxBch 28. K–B2 BxQ wins.

27. . . .	RxQ
28. QR–N1	P–B4
29. P–R6	P–B5
30. B–B6	P–B6ch
31. K–B2	RxR
32. RxR	K–B5

Threatening both 33. . . . B–Q5ch and 33. . . . P–K6ch.

33. R–N4	B–B6
34. R–B4	B–R4!
35. K–B1	B–N3
36. B–N7	P–R4
37. R–B6	P–K6!
38. R–B4ch	. . .

Or 38. RxB P–K7ch 39. K–K1 P–B7ch 40. KxP P–K8=Qch 41. K–N2 R–K7 mate.

| 38. . . . | K–N4 |
| **Resigns** | |

Ay, every inch a King.

—Shakespeare

White wins

An Endgame Study composed by Emanuel Lasker and G. C. Reichhelm, 1901.

1. K–N1! . . .

White must get his King to either KN5 or QN5 to win. And the only way to do that is to obtain the *distant opposition*; that is, there must be an odd number of squares between the Kings and it must be the opponent's turn to move.

If 1. K–N2? K–R1! 2. K–R2 K–N2! 3. K–N1 K–R2 4. K–B2 K–N1 5. K–Q2 K–B1! 6. K–Q3 K–B2 7. K–B3 K–N2! 8. K–B4 K–N3! 9. K–Q3 K–B2! 10. K–K3 K–Q2 and draws.

But from the diagram with the move Black can draw by 1. . . . K–N2! 2. K–N1 K–R2! 3. K–N1 K–R1! Or 3. K–B1 K–N2. Or 3. K–B2 K–N1.

1. . . . K–N2

If 1. . . . K–R1 2. K–N2! K–N2 3. K–B3! K–N3 4. K–B4! K–N2 5. K–N5 and wins.

2. K–B1 K–B2
3. K–Q1 K–Q2

If 3. . . . K–B1 4. K–Q2! K–B2 (4. . . . K–Q2 5. K–B3 K–B2 6. K–Q3 wins) 5. K–Q3 K–N2 6. K–K3 wins.

4. K–B2!	K–B1
5. K–Q2!	K–Q2
6. K–B3	K–B2
7. K–Q3!	K–N2

If 7. . . . K–Q2 8. K–B4 K–B2 9. K–N5 wins.

8. K–K3! and White wins

For if 8. . . . K–B2 9. K–B3 K–Q2 10. K–N3 K–K2 11. K–R4 K–B3 12. K–R5 K–N2 13. K–N5 wins.

The White King has outflanked his Black counterpart. This construction is the backbone of the "Theory of Corresponding Squares."

3	4	3	4	3	4	3	4
1	2	1	2	1	2	1	2
3	4	3	4	3	4	3	4
1	2	1	2	1	2	1	2
3	4	3	4	3	4	3	4
1	2	1	2	1	2	1	2
3	4	3	4	3	4	3	4
1	2	1	2	1	2	1	2

An understanding of the "Theory of Corresponding Squares" provides a player with a yardstick for calculating which side has, can obtain, or loses the *opposition*. For example (see the above diagram), when enemy Kings are standing on squares marked with the same number anywhere on the board, the side whose turn it is to move loses the *opposition*.

For some Kings the shortest distance between two points is not a straight line.

White draws

An Endgame Study composed by Richard Reti, 1921.

1. K–N7! . . .

The King begins to zigzag its way into the game. If 1. K–R7?? P–R5 wins. And if 1. P–B7?? K–N2 wins.

1. . . . **P–R5**

On 1. . . . K–N3 2. K–B6 (threatening 3. K–N5) P–R5 4. K–K5! (this is the critical intersection square) 4. . . . P–R6 (if 4. . . . KxP 5. K–B4 draws) 5. K–Q6 P–R7 6. P–B7 P–R8=Q (6. . . . K–N2 7. K–Q7 P–R8=Q 8. P–B8=Qch draws) 8. P–B8=Q draws.

2. K–B6! **P–R6**
3. K–K6! . . .

Albeit by necessity, the King changes his mind and chooses his alternative option.

3. . . . **P–R7**
4. P–B7 **P–R8=Q**
5. P–B8=Qch . . .

And draws. A miraculous theme which is known as "extended triangulation."

The Queen

The powers of the Queen are exceptional, combining both the long-range vertical and horizontal strength of the Rook with the across-the-board diagonal capacity of the Bishop. With a value of almost two Rooks, or three minor pieces, or nine pawns, its fantastic mobility, its lightning-quick changes of front, and its unbounded ability to give checks from all angles, it is the ideal attacking piece, operating with equal effect against pawn weaknesses, insecure pieces, or an exposed King. A piece whose action is predominantly tactical, its very presence often exerts decisive influence on the strategical nature of the position. And in the ending it defies schema, makes its own rules: Queen-and-pawn endings are particularly difficult, and Queen-and-Knight against Queen-and-Knight endings create fanciful situations. So strong and highly regarded is the Queen that its loss nearly always means the loss of the game. Many beginners even believe an exchange of Queens is a fatal blow!

Mate-in-three
—with three different Queen moves.

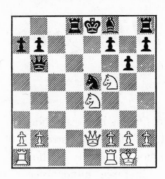

White to move

Alekhine–Kussman, New York 1924.

| **1. Q–N5ch!** | N–Q2 |

If 1. . . . QxQ 2. N–B6 mate.

| **2. KR–K1** | 2. . . . |

Threatening 3. N–B6 mate.

2. . . .	B–N5
3. N–B6ch	K–B1
4. NxNch	RxN
5. Q–K5!	Resigns

There is no defense against the three mates menaced by the Queen: 6. Q–K8 mate, 6. Q–N7 mate, and 6. QxR mate!

The Queen is offered three ways, and White cannot accept the offer in any form.

—Marshall

After 23. R–QB5

Levitsky–Marshall, Breslau 1912.

23. . . .   **Q–KN6!!!**

"The most elegant move I have ever played!" wrote Marshall. And perhaps the most elegant one *anybody* has ever played! The immediate threat is 24. . . . QxRP mate.

Resigns

There is no defense. The variations are fascinating:

A. 24. QxQ N–K7ch 25. K–R1 NxQch 26. K–N1 (if 26. BPxN RxR mate) NxR 27. PxR N–Q7 and Black wins with a clear piece ahead.

B. 24. Q–K5 N–B6ch 25. K–R1 RxP mate.

C. 24. BPxQ N–K7ch 25. K–R1 RxR mate.

D. 24. RPxQ N–K7 mate.

In his book *My Fifty Years of Chess*, Marshall, who was champion of the United States for twenty-seven years, writes that this game so excited the spectators that they "showered me with gold pieces!"

The queene is quaint, and quicke conceit, which makes hir walke which way she list, and rootes them up, that lie in wait to worke hir treason, ere she wist: hir force is such, against hir foes, that whom she meetes, she overthrowes.

—Breton

After 28. . . . QxR

Marshall–Kashdan, New York 1929.

29. Q–K7ch		. . .

This is the first of thirteen checks with the Queen to overthrow her foe.

29. . . .		**K–N3**
30. **Q–K8ch**		**K–R2**

If 30. . . . R–B2 31. Q–N8ch wins.

31. Q–Q7ch		. . .

31. Q–R8ch roots them up more rapidly.

31. . . .		**K–N3**
32. **Q–K8ch**		**K–R2**
33. **Q–R8ch**		**K–N3**
34. **Q–K8ch**		**K–R2**
35. **Q–R8ch**		**K–N3**
36. **Q–N8ch**		. . .

White has found the way.

| 36. . . . | K–R4 |
| 37. Q–K8ch | K–N5 |

On 37. . . . K–R5 White wins the Queen with 38. B–B6ch.

38. Q–N6ch	K–R5
39. B–B6ch	RxB
40. P–N3ch!	K–R6
41. Q–R5 mate	

The powers of the Queen are extraordinary.
—Fine

After 18. . . . R–Q1

Marshall–Gladstone, New York 1932.

19. Q–R7ch	K–B1
20. Q–R8ch	K–K2
21. QxNP!	. . .

This is the point of the checks.

| 21. . . . | QxPch |
| 22. K–R1 | BxB |

Forced, for if 22. . . . Q–Q5 23. N–K4 wins.

| 23. QxPch | K–Q3 |
| 24. N–K4ch | K–Q4 |

If 24. . . . K–K4 25. Q–N7ch K–Q4 26. KR–Q1ch forces mate.

| 25. Q–R5ch | B–N4 |

If 25. . . . P–K4 26. Q–B7ch wins. And if 25. . . . N–K4 26. KR–Q1ch wins.

| 26. Q–Q1ch! | . . . |

Back to the Queenside again!

| 26. . . . | Q–Q5 |

If 26. . . . K–K4 27. Q–Q6 mate.

27. Q–N3ch	K–K4
28. Q–N3ch	K–Q4
29. Q–Q6 mate	

The main characteristic of the Queen is its great mobility.

—Pachman

After Black's 17th

Bogolyubov–Mieses, Baden-Baden 1925.

18. Q–N2!	. . .

Threatening to prevent Black from castling with 19. Q–N4.

18. . . .	O–O
19. Q–R3	KR–Q1

If 19. . . . NPxP 20. Q–Q6 KR–Q1 21. R–N1 B–K1 22. Q–B7 KR–B1 23. Q–K7 with winning pressure by White.

20. PxNP	PxP
21. Q–R6!	. . .

Menacing 22. BxP! PxB?? 23. QxQ.

21. . . .	Q–R4

Some better is 21. . . . Q–R5, covering KB3 and threatening 22. . . . QxBP/7.

22. BxP!	PxB
23. RxPch!	. . .

White gives away his pieces—for good reason!

23. . . .	KxR

If 23. . . . K–R1 24. Q–KB6 mates in three.

24. Q–B6ch	K–N1
25. R–N1ch!	Q–N5
26. RxQch	PxR
27. P–B5	. . .

Now the two connected passed pawns prove decisive.

27. . . .	KR–QB1
28. P–K6	B–B3
29. Q–B7ch	K–R1
30. P–B6	R–KN1
31. Q–B7	QR–QB1
32. Q–K5	P–Q5ch
33. K–N1	Resigns

If 33. . . . P–Q6 34. P–B7ch R–N2 35. P–K7 wins.

Pawn snatching with the Queen is an art
—when it succeeds.

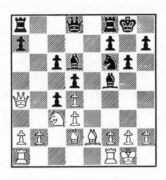

After 13. . . . B–Q3

Kavalek–Calvo, Montilla 1976.

14. QxP/6	. . .

The first snatch.

14. . . .	**R–N1**
15. P–QN3	**R–N3**

If 15. . . . PxP 16. PxP RxP 17. RxP.

16. Q–R4	**B–Q2**
17. Q–R5!	. . .

But not the immediate snatch 17. QxRP? because Black could then force a draw by repetition with 17. . . . B–B1 (threatening to win the Queen with 18. . . . R–R3) 18. Q–R4 R–R3 19. Q–N5 R–R4 20. Q–B6 R–R3.

17. . . .	**B–QN5**
18. QxRP!	. . .

But now the second snatch is safe.

18. . . .	**B–B1**
19. PxP	**R–R3**
20. Q–N8!	. . .

This is the only safe square, but one is enough.

      20. . . .   **Q–R4**

Threatening to win a piece with 21. . . . B–N5 or 21. . . . BxN.

      21. PxP!   **BxN**

If 21. . . . B–N5 22. Q–N5!

      22. BxB   **QxB**
      23. QR–B1!   **Q–Q7**
      24. RxB   **Resigns**

After 24. . . . RxR 25. QxRch K–N2 26. QxR, White is a Rook ahead. And after 24. . . . QxB (24. . . . N–Q2 25. RxRch K–N2 26. Q–N5 wins) 25. RxRch K–N2 26. P–Q6, he is the Exchange and three pawns ahead.

Endgames with Queen and pawns on both sides are among the most difficult in chess.

                           —Keres

White to move

Gligoric–German, Skopje 1972.

      1. P–QN4!   **. . .**

Forcing the Queen away from its passed pawn.

| 1. . . . | Q–QB1 |

If 1. . . . Q–Q4 (or 1. . . . Q–B5) 2. Q–B8ch Q–N1 3. Q–B6ch Q–N2 4. Q–Q8ch Q–N1 5. QxPch wins. And if 1. . . . Q–B6??? 2. Q–B8 mate.

| 2. QxPch | K–N1 |
| 3. P–QR4 | . . . |

Now that material superiority has been established, the next step is to fix the Queenside pawns.

3. . . .	Q–B2
4. P–N5	K–B2
5. P–B4!	. . .

Second step: the advance of the "candidate."

| 5. . . . | K–K3 |

It won't go far!

| 6. K–B2! | . . . |

Third step: the activation of the King.

| 6. . . . | K–B2 |
| 7. K–N3 | P–KR4? |

More resistant, but unavailing, is 7. . . . K–K3 8. K–N4 K–B2 9. Q–Q5ch K–B1 10. Q–K5 Q–Q2ch 11. K–N5 K–N1 12. P–N4 Q–Q1ch 13. Q–B6 and White wins.

| 8. Q–Q5ch | K–B1 |

If 8. . . . K–B3 9. Q–N5ch K–B2 10. Q–K5 Q–B5 11. K–R4 wins.

9. Q–K5!	Q–B2
10. K–R4	K–N1
11. K–N5	K–R2
12. P–B5!	Resigns

The fourth and final step, the breakthrough with the King, Queen, and Bishop pawn, is decisive. If 12. . . . PxP (12. . . .

Q–N1 13. Q–K7ch wins) 13. QxPch QxQch 14. KxQ K–R4 15. P–R4 wins.

Pawn promotions are frequently an integral part of Queen and pawn endings.

Black to move

De Lange–Hübner, Eckenforde 1974.

1. . . .   **P–B6!**

Establishing a strong point at K7 and creating certain mating threats on the eighth rank.

2. **P–N5**   **P–R5**

Second Queens offer the only winning chances.

3. **P–N6**   **P–R6**
4. **Q–Q7**   **Q–K4ch!**
5. **K–Q2**   **P–R7!**
6. **Q–R3ch**   **K–N4**
7. **P–N7**   . . .

Not 7. QxBP? Q–N7ch 8. K–Q1 Q–N8ch and Black wins.

7. . . .	Q–Q5ch
8. K–B1	Q–B6ch!
9. K–Q1	Q–Q6ch
10. K–B1	QxPch
11. K–Q2	Q–N7ch
12. K–Q3	Q–K7ch
13. K–B3	Q–K8ch
14. K–Q3	P–R8=Q
15. QxQ	. . .

If 15. Q–N3ch K–B4 16. P–N8=Q Q–K5ch 17. K–B3 Q–B8ch 18. K–N3 Q/5–B5 mate.

15. . . .	QxQ
16. P–N8=Q	Q–B8ch
17. K–K4	. . .

If 17. K–Q4, 17. K–B2, or 17. K–Q2, then 17. . . . QxPch wins. If 17. K–K3 Q–K7ch 18. K–Q4 QxPch wins. And if 17. K–B3 QxP 18. Q–K5ch K–N5 and Black eventually gets out of check and queens his BP.

17. . . .	Q–K7ch
18. K–Q5	QxP
Resigns	

The real sacrifice of the Queen is never a full but a partial sacrifice.

—Spielmann

After 21. . . . P–B3

Szmetan–Garcia, Costa del Sol 1976.

22. Q–R5!   . . .

There is nothing in chess more thrilling than a Queen sacrifice.

22. . . .   **N–Q6ch**

An attempt to deflect one of the Rooks.

If 22. . . . R–R1 23. Q–R6ch K–N1 24. PxP NxP 25. PxB NxB 26. RxPch! K–B2 (26. . . . PxR 27. QxP mate) 27. R–N7ch K–K1 28. Q–R5ch K–Q2 29. P–K8=Qch wins everything.

23. K–N1   **PxQ**
24. PxPch   **K–R1**

If 24. . . . K–R3 25. B–K3ch N–B5 26. RxN wins.

25. PxBch   **N–K4**
26. PxR=Qch   **RxQ**
27. RxP   **RxP**

Threatening 28. . . . R–B8 mate!

28. BxR   **Resigns**

For if 28. . . . Q–B5 29. RxN Q–B8ch 30. B–K1 and White wins.
And if 28. . . . N–B3 29. R–B5 Q–K2 30. R–B7 Q–K1 31. B–B5 and
the threat of 32. R–B8ch cannot be met.

Note the peculiar ascent—and descent—of White's Queen.

—Korn

White wins

An Endgame Study composed by B. S. Barrett, the *Dubuque
Chess Journal*, 1874.

1. Q–B3	K–N8
2. Q–Q3ch	. . .

The pin-and-check and pin-and-check two-step begin.

2. . . .	K–R8
3. Q–Q4	K–N8
4. Q–K4ch	K–R8
5. Q–K5	K–N8
6. Q–B5ch	K–R8
7. Q–B6	K–N8
8. Q–N6ch	K–R8
9. Q–N7	K–N8

10.	Q–R7ch	K–R8
11.	Q–R8!	. . .

Not 12. Q–R1ch?? P–N8=Q 13. Q–QB1 (13. Q–R8ch?? Q–N7ch
14. QxQch KxQ and Black wins) 13. . . . QxQch 14. KxQ stalemate!

11.	. . .	K–N8
12.	Q–R1 mate	

An amusing old favorite.

The Rook

The Rook, next to the Queen, is the most powerful piece. Valued at five pawns, or worth a little more than half a Queen and a little less than two minor pieces, it reaches across the whole board, vertically and horizontally, and, unless obstructed, it always has the choice of fourteen squares to which it can move. With a capacity for positional maneuvers, it also has considerable powers of attack, being able to menace several pieces placed on the same file or rank. Some call it an ox, some a battering ram, some an artillery piece. Masters love its predictability and logicality. Rook-and-pawn endings are among their favorites. But novices and beginners find it rather tedious, duller than the skipping Knight and the quick-attacking Bishop. A pity, fortunately soon overcome with the development of the player, but readily understood. The fact is that the Rooks enter the fray comparatively late: after castling, the development of the Queen, Bishops, and Knights, and three or four pawn moves. But once the pieces are mobilized, once pawns are advanced, once there have been exchanges of pieces and pawns, once files have been opened, and once the character of the position has been established, then the Rook comes into its own, dwarfing the minor pieces, seizing first files and then ranks, and largely dominating the future course of both the middlegame and ending.

With "a pig on the seventh" (Nimzovich), Capablanca eats pawns and mounts mating threats.

White to move

Capablanca–Tartakower, New York 1924.

1. K–N3!   . . .

White's Rook is ideally placed on the seventh rank, but it requires the King's help.

1. . . .   **RxPch**
2. K–R4   **R–B6**

If 2. . . . R–B8 3. K–R5!

3. P–N6   **RxPch**
4. K–N5   **R–K5**

If 4. . . . RxP 5. K–B6 K–K1 (5. . . . K–N1 6. R–Q7 and mate in two moves) 6. RxP! RxP 7. P–N7 R–KN5 8. RxP P–Q5 9. P–N8= Qch RxQ 10. R–R8ch K–Q2 11. RxR K–Q3 12. KxP K–Q4 13. R–Q8ch K–B5 14. K–K4 and wins.

5. K–B6!   . . .

Black's KBP provides a convenient shelter from checks.

5. . . .   **K–N1**

Or 5. . . . K–K1 6. RxP and wins.

6. R–N7ch	K–R1
7. RxP	R–K1
8. KxP!	. . .

A deflective pawn is picked off, and an attack on the QP is
begun.

8. . . .	R–K5
9. K–B6	R–B5ch
10. K–K5	R–N5
11. P–N7ch	K–N1

Or 11. . . . RxP 12. RxR KxR 13. KxP and the Queen pawn
becomes a Queen.

| 12. RxP | . . . |

The QP will not run away. If now 12. . . . R–N4ch 13. K–B6 wins.

| 12. . . . | R–N8 |
| 13. KxP, and White | won. |

Seventh-rank absolute.

—Nimzovich

White to move

Alekhine–Eliskases, Buenos Aires 1939.

1. K–N2	P–R4
2. R–R6!	. . .

First the Rook goes behind the passed pawn.

2. . . .	P–R5
3. R–R7	. . .

Then it assumes the seventh-rank absolute. Ideal Rook play!

3. . . .	P–R6
4. P–N4	. . .

With the Rook settled, the pawns begin to advance.

4. . . .	K–B1
5. P–N5	K–N1

Marking time. If 5. . . . R–R8 6. K–B3 P–R7 (threatening to draw with 7. . . . R–KN8 8. RxP RxP) 7. K–B4 wins (7. . . . R–KB8 8. RxP).

6. K–N3	R–R8
7. K–N4	R–N8ch

Or 7. . . . R–KB8 8. P–B4 and wins.

8. K–B5	R–N7
9. P–B4	P–R7
10. K–B6	Resigns

For if 10. . . . R–K7 11. R–R8ch R–K1 12. RxP wins. And if 10. . . . K–N1 11. P–N6 wins.

The Genesis of a Rook.

—Nimzovich

These are the stages of the Rook's activity: occupies the file, 13. R–K1 (occurs before the diagram); takes the seventh rank, 26. R–K7; doubles on the file, 27. QR–K1; makes room for the second

Rook, 28. R–N7; doubles on the seventh rank, 29. R/1–K7; and mounts a mating attack, 35. RxBP and 41. RxKNP.

After 25. . . . B–N3

Karpov–Uhlmann, Madrid 1973.

26. R–K7!	P–N3
27. QR–K1	P–R3
28. R–N7	R–Q3?!

Or 28. . . . R–B7 29. R/1–K7 RxP 30. B–K8 R–B1 31. K–R2! R/1–B7 32. K–N3! and White has a decisive advantage. Or 28. . . . R–B7 29. R/1–K7 K–B1! 30. R/K–Q7 and White has the upper hand.

29. R/1–K7	P–R4
30. PxP	BxP
31. P–KN4!	B–N3
32. P–B4!	. . .

This clinches it.

32. . . .	R–B8ch
33. K–B2	R–B7ch
34. K–K3	B–K5
35. RxBP	R–N3
36. P–N5	K–R2
37. R/B–K7	RxQNP
38. B–K8	R–N6ch

39.	K–K2	R–N7ch
40.	K–K1	R–Q3
41.	RxPch	K–R1
42.	R/KN7–K7	Resigns

If 42. . . . R–Q1 (White threatened 43. B–Q7) 43. P–N6 R–KR7 44. R–R7ch RxR 45. RxRch K–N1 46. B–B7ch K–B1 47. R–R8ch K–K2 48. RxR KxR 49. P–N7 B–R2 50. P–N8=Qch BxQ 51. BxB wins.

Reshevesky on Rooks: winning one and handling one.

Black to move

Kagan–Reshevsky, Petropolis 1973.

| 1. . . . | K–Q6! |

The only move to win. If 1. . . . P–K4 2. RxP K–B4! probably draws, but 2. . . . P–Q6? 3. R–Q6 favors White.

| 2. RxKP | K–B7! |

Not 2. . . . K–B5? 3. RxP P–Q6 4. R–Q6 R–B7 5. K–B3 and White wins.

| 3. R–Q6 | . . . |

Not 3. RxP P–Q6 4. R–Q6 P–Q7 5. RxPch KxR 6. P–N5 R–N6 7. P–R4 RxP and Black wins.

3. . . .	P–Q6
4. K–B3	K–B8!

If 4. . . . P–Q7?? 5. K–K2 and wins.

5. K–N4	. . .

If 5. K–K3 P–Q7ch 6. K–K2 R–B1 7. RxP R–K8ch and Black wins.

5. . . .	P–Q7
6. P–R4	. . .

Or 6. K–N5 R–QR6 7. KxP? R–R3 and Black wins.

6. . . .	K–B7
7. RxPch	KxR
8. K–N5	R–B3
9. P–B4	K–K6
10. P–B5	PxP
11. KxP	K–Q5
12. P–R5	K–Q4
13. P–N5	R–Q3

Black's King and Rook play is exemplary.

14. K–N5	K–K3!

If 14. . . . K–K4?? 15. P–R6 draws!

15. K–N6	R–Q8
16. P–R6	R–N8ch
17. K–R7	K–B2
Resigns	

Otherwise 18. P–N6 R–N8 19. K–R8 RxP 20. K–R7 R–KN3 21. K–R8 RxP mate.

If one Rook attacks a pawn whilst the other is doomed to passive defense, this creates a prerequisite for the actively placed side to win.

—Levenfish and Smyslov

After 49. . . . K–K2

Lombardy–Ree, U.S.A. vs. Holland, Haifa 1976.

50. P–Q4!   . . .

A strong move which activates the King, bids for a passed pawn, and threatens 51. PxP PxP 52. R–R6.

50.	. . .	R–B3
51.	R–R7ch	R–B2
52.	R–R5	PxP
53.	K–Q3	K–Q3
54.	KxP	R–B3
55.	R–N5!	. . .

By tempoing, White brings on zugzwang.

55.	. . .	P–R3
56.	R–R5	K–K3
57.	R–R8	K–Q3
58.	R–Q8ch	K–B2
59.	R–Q5	. . .

Active Rook.

59. . . .	P–R4
60. P–R4!	. . .

Not 60. P–B5? P–N4!

60. . . .	K–B3
61. P–B5	PxPch?

Black misses a chance for a probable theoretical draw with 61.
. . . P–N4! 62. PxPch KxP.

62. RxPch	K–N3
63. R–N5ch	K–R3
64. K–K5	R–B3

If 64. . . . R–B1 65. K–K6 followed by 66. RxBP wins.

65. R–Q5!	. . .

If 65. KxP R–B5.

65. . . .	R–B5
66. R–Q6ch	K–N2
67. R–Q4	R–B8

Or 67. . . . R–B4ch 68. R–Q5 K–B3 69. RxRch KxR 70. KxP K–N5
71. K–K4 KxP 72. P–B5 K–N6 73. P–B6 P–R5 74. P–B7 P–R6 75.
P–B8=Q P–R7 76. Q–B6 K–B7 77. Q–R1 and White wins.

68. KxP	K–B3
69. K–K5	K–B4
70. R–K4	Resigns

Black must pay a Rook for the BP.

All things being equal, the player will prevail who first succeeds in uniting the efforts of both Rooks in an important direction.

—Znosko-Borovsky

After 22. . . . K–Q1

Olafsson–Miles, Teesside 1976.

    23. R–Q1   . . .

Centralizing the Rook with the threat of 24. N–N6.

23. . . .	P–QN3
24. P–N5	R–R2
25. QR–B1	K–K1
26. R–B6	R/2–N2

Awkward but necessary.

    27. R/1–QB1   . . .

Doubling Rooks on the open file and threatening 28. R–B8ch RxR 29. RxR mate.

27. . . .	P–B3
28. R–K6ch	K–B1
29. R/6–B6	K–B2
30. K–K3	K–B1

Not 30. . . . N–B4? 31. NxNP!

31. P–N4!   . . .

In order to win, a second front must be opened.

31. . . .	P–R3
32. P–R4	K–B2
33. P–N5	RPxP
34. PxP	PxP

Now the Kingside pawns are fatally weakened, but White was
menacing 35. R–KN1 and 36. P–N6ch with stifling effect.

35. R–KN1	P–N5
36. RxKNP	. . .

Threatening 37. R/6–KN6 and 38. RxPch.

36. . . .	N–B3
37. R–N5	NxNch

If 37. . . . R–K1 38. NxP.

38. PxN	K–N1

If 38. . . . R–K1 39. K–K4 wins a pawn.

39. RxKP	R–KB2
40. P–B4	R/1–KB1
41. R–K4	R–B4
42. P–Q6	Resigns

With the QP marching and 43. RxP looming, Black has no
reason to go on.

The Rook wins against two connected passed pawns, in the absence of the Kings, if the pawns are not yet to the sixth rank.

Black to move

Sanz–Benko, Orense 1974.

1. . . .	R–Q6
2. K–B2	. . .

If 2. P–R5 P–K6 3. K–B2 R–Q7ch 4. K–B1 R–QR7 wins.

2. . . .	K–K6!
3. P–R5	R–Q7ch
4. K–N1	. . .

If 4. K–B1 P–Q6 wins.

4. . . .	K–B5!

To clear the path for the KP. But 4. . . . P–Q6 5. P–R6 R–KR7 6. P–R7 R–R1 7. P–N4 R–R1 8. R–Q7 K–K7 9. P–N5 and White has a distinct advantage.

5. R–Q8	. . .

If 5. P–R6? P–K6 gives Black the advantage.

5. . . .	P–K6
6. R–B8ch	K–N4!

If 6. . . . K–K4? 7. P–R6 P–K7 8. R–K8 (threatening 9. P–R7), and White wins.

7. P–R6   . . .

On either 7. R–K8? P–K7 8. P–R6 R–Q8ch 9. K–B2 P–K8=Q 10. RxQ RxR 11. P–N4 K–B5 12. P–N5 K–K6 or 7. K–B1? R–QR7 8. R–K8 P–K7 9. P–R6 P–Q6, Black has a decisive plus.

7.	. . .	**P–K7**
8.	**R–K8**	**R–Q8ch**
9.	**K–N2**	**P–K8=Q**
10.	**RxQ**	**RxR**
11.	**P–N4**	**P–Q6**
12.	**K–B3**	**R–QR8**
13.	**KxP**	. . .

Or 13. P–N5 R–R6ch 14. K–Q2 K–B5 (threatening 15. . . . K–K5 and 16. . . . R–R7) and Black wins.

13.	. . .	**RxP**
14.	**P–N5**	**R–Q3ch**
15.	**K–B3**	**K–B3**
16.	**P–B5**	**R–Q8**
	Resigns	

For if 17. P–N6 R–QN8 18. K–B4 K–K3 19. P–B6 RxP 20. K–B5 R–N8 wins. Or if 17. K–N4 K–K3 18. K–R5 K–Q2 19. K–N6 K–B1 20. K–B6 R–KR8 21. P–N6 R–R4 wins.

Isolating the opponent's King from the passed pawn and then advancing the pawn is the correct strategy in such positions.

—Levenfish and Smyslov

Black to move

Janosevic–Minev, Uljma 1976.

| 1. . . . | R–R6! |

Laterally isolating the King from the passed pawn, preventing 2. P–R4, protecting his RP, and threatening 2. . . . RxP.

2. R–N7ch	K–Q3
3. R–N6ch	K–B4
4. RxP	P–Q5!

Not 4. . . . RxP? 5. K–N3 R–R8 6. K–N2 R–N8 7. R–B7 P–R3 8. R–B7ch! (if 8. R–B6 R–N3 is to Black's advantage) 8. . . . K–Q5 9. R–B6 K–K5 10. R–K6ch K–B5 11. R–B6ch and draws.

| 5. R–B7 | . . . |

Or 5. K–K4 R–K3ch 6. K–B4 R–K8 and wins.

| 5. . . . | K–B5 |
| 6. K–K4 | P–Q6! |

On 6. . . . R–K6ch 7. K–B4 R–K8 8. R–B7ch K–N6 9. RxP levels.

| 7. R–B2 | . . . |

Or 7. R–B7ch K–N6 and wins.

| 7. . . . | R–R3! |

Best. With 7. . . . K–B6?! 8. R–R2 P–Q7 9. R–R3ch K–N7 10. RxR P–Q8=Q 11. K–B4 White obtains counterplay.

| 8. P–N5 | R–K3ch |
| 9. K–B3 | . . . |

Or 9. K–B5 R–K7 10. R–B1 P–Q7 11. R–Q1 RxP and Black wins.

9. . . .	K–B6
10. P–R4	P–Q7
11. RxP	KxR
12. P–R5	R–K8
13. K–B4	R–B8ch
14. K–N4	. . .

Or 14. K–K5 R–KR8 and wins.

| 14. . . . | K–K6 |
| Resigns | |

After 15. P–N6 PxP 16. PxP (16. P–R6 R–B4 wins) K–K5 17. K–N5 K–K4 18. K–R6 (18. P–N7 R–N8ch 19. K–R6 K–B3 wins) 18. . . . K–B3 19. K–R7 R–R8ch Black mates in three moves.

Endings with Rooks and pawns are, together with pawn endings, the very essence of endgame play.

—Znosko-Borovsky

White to move

Maric–Petrovic, Yugoslavia 1974.

1. RxP	R–QB2
2. R–QB5	K–R4
3. R–B2!	K–R5
4. R–B1	K–R4

Or 4. . . . P–R4 5. R–B4! P–N5 6. RPxP PxP 7. R–B5! P–N6 8. PxPch PxP 9. K–N1! and White wins.

5. P–R4!!	P–N5

If 5. . . . KxP?? 6. R–R1 mate. And if 5. . . . PxP 6. K–R2 threatening 7. R–B5ch.

6. PxPch	KxNP
7. P–B3ch	KxP
8. R–B5	R–N2ch

If 8. . . . P–R4 9. K–B2 wins.

9. K–B1!	R–QB2
10. K–B2	P–R4

| 11. K–N2 | R–N2ch |
| 12. K–B1 | R–N7 |

If 12. . . . R–QB2 13. K–B2 and Black is in zugzwang.

13. RxPch   **Resigns**

On 13. . . . KxR 14. KxR and the QBP queens. 13. KxR?? would have stalemated!

A petty duel between two Rooks, with quite a few thematic points.

—**Korn**

White wins

An Endgame Study composed by Nicolas Rossolimo, *Kasseler Post* 1950.

1. P–R7   . . .

Threatening 2. R–R8 and 3. P–R8=Q.

2. . . .   **R–R3**

Tying the White Rook to its pawn and trying for 3. . . . P–N4.

2. K–N5!   . . .

With this and the next four moves the threat is to check and then to queen the pawn.

2. . . .	K–N6
3. K–B5	K–B6
4. K–Q5	K–Q6
5. K–K5	K–K6
6. K–B5	K–B6
7. R–KB8!!	. . .

A battery, as it is known in the world of problem and endgame composition.

7. . . .	RxP

Forced.

8. K–N6ch	K–N6
9. KxR	P–N4
10. K–N6!	P–N5
11. K–N5	K–R6
12. R–R8ch	K–N6
13. R–R4 and wins.	

The Bishop

"The Bishop is better than the Knight!" This statement is sure to spark a heated argument in any chess group. There are staunch advocates of both pieces. But ever since William Steinitz, "The Thinker," most authorities have in general favored the Bishop. It whisks across the whole board in only one move, whereas it takes the Knight four. It excels in open positions, unhindered by pawns. About the two Bishops, opposed by either Bishop and Knight or two Knights, there is little doubt. In all but exceptional cases they are recognized as superior and usually even constitute a winning advantage. Only in blocked positions or in positions where it is restricted by its own pawns must the Bishop defer to the Knight. So, according to Steinitz, having a Bishop for a Knight is to be ahead by "the Minor Exchange."

Two Bishops against Bishop and Knight con-stitute a tangible advantage.

—**Fine**

After 14. Q–B2

Rosenthal–Steinitz, Vienna 1873.

| 14. . . . | N–B5! |

Obtaining the two Bishops or forcing White to lose time and space.

15. BxN	QxB
16. Q–B2	P–QB4
17. N–B3	P–N3
18. N–K5	Q–K3
19. Q–B3	B–QR3
20. KR–K1	P–B3
21. N–N4	P–R4

The Knight is deprived of every good outpost.

22. N–B2	Q–B2
23. P–B5?	P–KN4
24. QR–Q1	B–N2!

Winning the best diagonal on the board.

25. Q–N3	R–Q4!
26. RxR	QxR
27. R–Q1	. . .

Either the KBP or the QRP must go.

27. . . .	QxBP
28. Q–B7	B–Q4
29. P–QN3	R–K1
30. P–B4	B–B2
31. B–B1	. . .

If 31. R–K1 (31. B–Q2 R–K7) RxB 32. RxR Q–N8ch 33. N–Q1 QxNch wins.

31. . . .	R–K7!
32. R–B1	Q–B7

Threatening to win two pieces for a Rook with 33. . . . RxN 34. RxR QxBch.

33. Q–N3	QxRP
Resigns	

Sometimes a bad Bishop can be converted into a good Bishop.

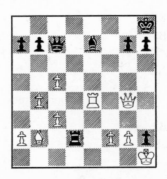

White to move

Capablanca–Spielmann, San Sebastian 1911.

        1. B–B1   . . .

Attacked and hemmed in by its own pawns, the Bishop finds a way to join its fellow pieces on the Kingside.

        1. . . .   **RxBP**

Threatening 2. . . . R–B8 mate.

        2. B–B4   . . .

Defends against mate, attacks the Queen, and begins a mating attack on the eighth rank.

        2. . . .   **Q–Q1**

Having to defend both the first rank and the Bishop, the Queen is overloaded.

        3. RxB   **Q–KB1**

If 3. . . . QxR 4. Q–B8ch Q–B1 5. QxQ mate.

        4. QxPch   **QxQ**
        5. R–K8ch   **Q–N1**

Or 5. . . . Q–B1 6. RxQch K–N2 7. B–R6ch KxB 8. RxR and wins.

        6. B–K5ch   **R–B3**
        7. BxR mate

A metamorphosis!

A "Bishop and a half" can easily become two— and seem like two and a half.

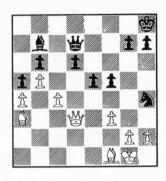

After 27. BxN

Portisch–Larsen, Las Palmas 1976.

White has just obtained the two Bishops, but he is a pawn behind and one of the Bishops is only potentially strong. The QB, however, is such a powerhouse that it recharges its fellow.

27. . . .	P–Q4
28. PxP	BxP

If 28. . . . QxQP 29. QxQ BxQ 30. B–Q6 B–N6 31. B–B7 BxP 32. BxNP B–B7 33. BxP and White wins.

29. Q–K3	P–K5

If 29. . . . Q–QB2 30. B–N2 N–N3 31. P–R4! P–B5 (or 31. . . . NxP 32. QxKP QxQ 33. BxQ and White wins by capturing the QNP and QRP and advancing his own QNP) 32. Q–B3 QxQ 33. BxQ P–R4 34. B–Q3 B–B2 (if 34. . . . NxP 35. BxKP wins) 35. BxRP!! PxB 36. BxN B–Q4 (if 36. . . . BxB 37. P–N6 wins) 37. B–K4! and White wins. A brilliant variation!

30. PxP	BxP
31. QxP	. . .

White has regained his pawn and has a winning position.

| 31. . . . | P–R3 |
| 32. Q–Q6 | Q–B1 |

Black cannot afford to exchange Queens.

| 33. B–N2 | . . . |

Threatening 34. QxPch K–N1 35. QxN.

| 33. . . . | K–R2 |
| 34. Q–K7 | . . . |

Menacing both mate and the Knight.

34. . . .	Q–KN1
35. QxN	Q–R7
36. Q–B2	QxP
37. Q–R7	Resigns

Three diagonals, one for the Queen and two for the Bishops, are worth a pawn.

After 21. . . . QxP

Taimanov–Kholmov, Suhumi 1972.

22. R–B4! . . .

Threatening 23. R–KN4.

| 22. . . . | P–K4 |

This closes Black's KR1–QR8 diagonal to White's Bishop but weakens his KN1–QR7 diagonal and the KB4-square.

23. N–R4	P–N3
24. R–Q1	Q–B3
25. B–Q5!	. . .

Seizing the third diagonal and threatening 26. QxPch or 26. NxP.

| 25. . . . | P–KN4 |
| 26. R–Q3! | N–Q5 |

If 26. . . . PxN 27. R–KB3 wins.

| 27. RxR | BxB |

If 27. . . . BxR 28. BxN PxB 29. R–KB3 gives White a decisive advantage.

| 28. RxRch | QxR |
| 29. BxN | B–K5 |

After 29. . . . PxB 30. RxP Black remains the Exchange down.

| 30. BxKP | . . . |

Opening the QR1–KR8 diagonal again and threatening 31. RxN QxR 32. QxB PxN 33. Q–R8ch with a mating attack.

30. . . .	Q–K1
31. B–N2	BxR
32. QxB	PxN
33. Q–Q4	. . .

Finally winning a pawn by the threat of mate.

33. . . .	P–B3
34. QxRP	Q–K8ch
35. K–N2	N–K4
36. P–KR3	K–N2
37. Q–KB4	Q–Q8
38. Q–K4	Q–Q3

39. Q–N7ch	K–N3
40. Q–R8	K–B4
41. BxN	KxB
42. P–B4ch!	Resigns

For if 42. . . . K–Q5 43. K–B3 and if 42. . . . K–B4 or 42. . . . K–K3 43. Q–B8ch with a won Queen-and-pawn ending in each case.

Bishops are better than Knights in open positions.

After 46. . . . K–B1

Lombardy–Weisskohl, New York 1976.

White sacrificed a pawn to reach this position in which the two Bishops dominate the whole board.

47. P–K5	N–N2
48. B–K4	N–Q1
49. P–B5	. . .

Gaining additional space and preventing 49. . . . N–K3 and 49. . . . P–N3.

49. . . .	K–K2
50. K–Q3	K–Q2
51. P–R6	P–N3

Black is desperate for a move.

	52. PxP	PxP
	53. BxP	P–B4

If 53. . . . K–K3 54. K–K4 followed by 55. B–B5ch.

| | 54. B–B5ch | K–K2 |

Or 54. . . . N–K3 55. K–B4 K–K2 56. K–Q5 and White wins.

| | 55. B–R4ch | K–K1 |
| | 56. P–K6 | . . . |

Threatening 57. B–N6ch K–B1 58. P–K7ch.

	56. . . .	N–B3
	57. K–B4	N–K2
	58. B–K4	K–B1
	59. B–KB2	Resigns

After 60. BxP one of the White passed pawns would prevail. An excellent example of how the combined power of two Bishops and passed pawns overcomes a Bishop, Knight, and passed pawns.

A fianchetto with a Bishop is better than a fianchetto without a Bishop.

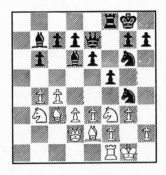

After 18. P–N3

Fraguela–Larsen, Las Palmas 1976.

With a powerfully fianchettoed Queen Bishop, Black sets out to exploit the absence of White's Bishop from KN2.

18. . . .   **P–R4!**

Threatening 19. . . . P–R5 and the opening of the KR-file.

19. P–B5   . . .

A diversion. If 19. P–R4? NxRP! 20. NxN QxN! 21. PxQ B–R7 mate!

19. . . .   **PxP**
20. PxP   **BxBP!**

Sacrifices the Exchange to activate the Queen.

21. P–R3?   . . .

Less weakening is 21. NxB QxN 22. B–N4 Q–Q4 23. BxR N/3–K4 24. Q–Q1 KxB 25. P–R3 N–KB3 26. K–N2.

21. . . .	**N–B3**
22. NxB	**QxN**
23. B–N4	**Q–Q4**
24. BxR	**N–K4**
25. P–K4	**NxKP!**
26. Q–K3	. . .

Or 26. PxN NxNch 27. BxN QxQ and Black wins.

26. . . .   **N–Q7!!**
Resigns

Nothing can be done. If 27. QxN/Q NxNch 28. BxN QxB and Black mates at KN7 or KR8. If 27. QxN/K NxNch 28. BxN QxQ wins. If 27. R–Q1 (27. NxN/Q or 27. NxN/K Q–N7 mate) 27. . . . N/7xNch wins.

And if 27. B–N4 N/4xNch 28. BxN NxBch 29. K–R1 N–Q7ch 30. P–B3 NxR 31. Q–B2 QxPch 32. QxQ BxQch 33. K–N1 B–K7, and Black has an overwhelming material advantage.

A pinned Knight is always wholly pinned.
—Nimzovich

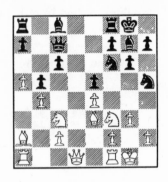

After 14. B–K3

Grefe–Rohde, Lone Pine 1976.

| 14. . . . | B–N5 |

A common, albeit deadly, pin in the opening.

| 15. Q–K2 | . . . |

"Putting the question" (P–KR3) to the Bishop is not all that
easy, for if 15. K–N2 Q–B1 16. R–R1 B–R6ch 17. K–N1 P–KR3
and the different question of what to do with KR has arisen.

| 15. . . . | P–KR3 |
| 16. KR–Q1 | . . . |

Necessary to break the pin is the maneuver 16. B–B5 KR–K1
17. Q–K3.

| 16. . . . | N–R2 |
| 17. P–R4 | . . . |

Forced.

17. . . .	P–N4!
18. PxP	N–B5!!
19. PxN	PxBP
20. B–B5	NxP

Increased pressure on the pinned Knight produces threats to win material and threats to mate.

21. R–Q3   . . .

If 21. BxR BxN (or 21. . . . NxNch) 22. B–Q6 Q–B1 23. Q–B1 Q–N5ch and Black mates in two.

21. . . .	KR–Q1
22. R/1–Q1	NxNch
23. RxN	BxN!
24. R–N3	. . .

Too late the pin is broken!

24. . . .	PxR
25. QxBch	K–R1
26. RxRch	RxR
27. Q–B3	PxPch
28. BxP	B–N2
29. QxP	QxQ
30. BxQ	B–Q5
Resigns	

Do not place your pawns on the color of your Bishop.

—Fine

After 24. . . . K–N1

Diesen–Shamkovich, New York 1976.

25. R–B7	. . .

Black's pawns, bar one, are all on the wrong color squares. And to make matters worse, White controls the QB-file and the seventh rank with his Rook and most of the dark squares with his Bishop.

25. . . .	P–N3
26. P–QR4	B–R3
27. R–R3	KR–B1
28. R/3–QB3	RxR
29. RxR	R–QB1

Black struggles to exchange all the Rooks and obtain a drawn ending with Bishops of opposite colors.

30. RxRP	RxP
31. P–R4	B–B1
32. P–QN4	. . .

Playing for a passed pawn.

32. . . .	K–B1
33. B–Q8	P–K4

Some material for a little freedom and a passed QP. But it does not help.

34. BxP	PxP
35. BxP	R–B8ch
36. K–R2	R–B5
37. B–B5ch	K–N2

If 37. . . . K–K1 38. R–K7ch K–Q1 39. RxP wins, and if 37. . . . K–N1 38. R–R8 wins.

38. R–B7	B–K3
39. P–R5	P–Q5
40. P–R6	P–Q6
41. R–B6!	RxPch
42. K–N1	R–R4

If 42. . . . P–Q7 43. R–Q6 wins.

43. B–Q4ch   **P–B3**

Or 43. . . . K–B1 44. P–R7 wins. Or 43. . . . K–R3 44. B–K3ch wins.

44. RxB   **R–Q4**
45. B–K3   **Resigns**

After 45. . . . P–Q7 46. BxP RxB 47. P–N5 R–R7 48. R–K7ch, White queens one of his passed pawns.

The Bishop is the best defender of a weak-color complex.

After 18. . . . RxP

Soltis–Quinteros, Cleveland 1975.

19. Q–R4!   **. . .**

This forces Black to part with his KB and thereby bring about the weak-color complex: the dark squares around the King.

19. . . .   **BxN**

If 19. . . . P–KR4 20. BxRP! BxN 21. QxB PxB 22. QxPch K–N2 23. Q–N5ch K–R2 24. R–B3 and White mates in two.

| 20. QxB | N–N2? |

After 20. . . . RxP! it is not clear how White wins.

21. B–B5	R–K1
22. B–K7	K–N1
23. B–B6	. . .

Making Black really hurt on the dark squares.

| 23. . . . | R/1–N1 |
| 24. B–N4! | . . . |

Menacing 25. Q–R6 N–K1 (25. . . . N–B4? 26. BxN wins) 26. B–K7 N–N2 27. B–Q6 winning the Exchange.

24. . . .	N–K1
25. B–K7	Q–B1
26. R–R3!	R–N8
27. B–Q1	. . .

Ruling out any chances Black might have on his eighth rank.

27. . . .	P–QR4
28. Q–R6	N–N2
29. R–R3	Resigns

On 29. . . . N–R4, White mates appropriately on a dark square with 30. RxN PxR 31. Q–N5ch K–R1 32. B–B6.

The Bishop   67

Many a Bishop has dominated many a castle.

White wins

An Endgame Study composed by J. E. Peckover, Szachy 1957.

      1. B–N6   . . .

Threatening to win easily with 2. B–N2.

      1. . . .   **P–N7**
      2. B–N5!   . . .

If 2. BxP? RxB 3. P–B7 R–R7ch 4. K–N6 R–R1 5. K–N7 R–KN1 draws. The text threatens 3. B–N1.

      2. . . .   **P–N8=Q**
      3. BxQ   **RxB**

Now if the pawn can be captured . . .

      4. P–B7   **R–R8ch**
      5. K–N6   **R–R1**

Or 5. . . . R–N8ch 6. K–B6 and Black has no check at QB8.

      6. K–N7   **R–KB1!**

If 6. . . . R–K1 or 6. . . . R–KN1, 7. B–Q8 wins.

      7. B–K7   . . .

Step by step the Bishop deprives the Rook of vital squares, always with the threat of B–Q8 allowing the pawn to queen.

7. . . .   **R–KN1**

If 7. . . . R–K1 8. B–Q8 and the Rook is cut off from QB1 and cannot pin the pawn with 8. . . . R–K2.

8. **B–Q8**   . . .

Threatening 9. P–B8=Q.

8. . . .   **R–N2**

9. **B–B6 and wins.**

Because of 10. BxR(ch) and 11. P–B8=Q(ch).

The Knight

The Knight has been described as "the terror of the tyro." And not without good reason. Its characteristics are unique. It can jump over pieces and pawns, its own and its opponent's; it moves in a queer L-shaped fashion, from a white square to a black square and then back to a white one, and so on; it zigzags forward, backward, and sideways, and its destination is almost unpredictable. It can attack any other piece without itself being in immediate danger from that piece. Forking is its deadly business. And, when centrally posted, protected from attack by enemy pieces and pawns, reaching out to eight squares, in closed, blocked positions, it is in its glory and often exerts as much power as a Rook.

But there is a darker side to the Knight. It is a short-range piece, requiring four moves to cross the board. Decentralized in a corner, it covers only two squares. It cuts a poor figure at stopping enemy passed pawns or at defending a vulnerable one of its own. Two Knights cannot force mate, whereas a Queen, a Rook, or two Bishops can. Badly placed, it is a definite weakness and prompts the old sayings: "A Knight on the side brings only trouble" or "A Knight on the rim is dim!"

The Knight, lacking the Bishop's long range, takes much more time to stop or to win a pawn.
—Znosko-Borovsky

White to move

Marshall–Capablanca, New York 1927.

      1. N–K4   . . .

With the QBP indefensible, counterplay against the Queenside pawns must be sought.

      1. . . .   **NxP**
      2. N–Q6   **N–K6!**
      3. P–QR4   . . .

If 3. NxNP N–B5 winning either the QRP or the QNP.

      3. . . .   **N–Q4!**

If 3. . . . P–QN3 4. N–B8!

      4. NxNP   . . .

On 4. P–B5 or 5. P–KN3, Black replies 4. . . . P–QN3.

      4. . . .   **NxP**
      5. P–QN4   . . .

With 5. K–N1 K–B1 6. P–KN3 (6. K–B2? N–Q6ch wins) N–Q6 7. P–N3 White offers more, though insufficient, resistance.

5. . . .	N–Q4
6. P–N5	N–B6!
7. N–R5	. . .

White's plan is to exchange QRPs. If 7. N–B5, Black wins by . . .
K–B1, . . . K–K2, and . . . K–Q3.

7. . . .	NxRP
8. N–B6	K–B1
9. NxP	K–K2

The entrance of the Black King guarantees victory.

10. N–B6ch	K–Q3
11. K–N1	P–B3

Before going after the QNP, Black safeguards his own pawns.

12. K–B2	P–K4
13. N–Q8	K–Q2!
14. N–N7	. . .

After 15. N–B7 K–K2 16. N–R8 P–N4 the White Knight is completely out of play.

14. . . .	K–B2
15. N–R5	N–B6
16. K–B3	NxP
17. K–K4	N–Q3ch
18. K–Q5	K–Q2
19. N–B6	N–B4
20. N–N8ch	K–K2
21. N–B6ch	K–B2
22. N–Q8ch	. . .

Or 22. K–K4 N–K2 and Black wins.

22. . . .	K–K1
Resigns	

Two extra pawns are too much. If 23. N–K6 K–K2 24. N–B5
N–K6ch 25. K–K4 NxP makes it simple for Black.

One piece (the Knight) wins this game practically single-handed!

—**Chernev**

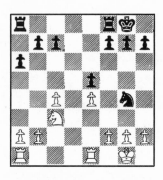

After 15. . . . PxQ

Tarrasch–Vogel, Nuremburg 1910.

16. N–Q5!	P–QB3

Comparatively better is 16. . . . N–B3?! accepting doubled KBPs. For after 17. NxP QR–B1 and Black regains the pawn with counterplay. The text seriously weakens Q3.

17. N–K7ch	K–R1
18. N–B5	QR–Q1
19. QR–Q1	P–KN3
20. N–Q6	. . .

A new and stronger outpost. The threat is 21. NxPch winning the Exchange.

20. . . .	R–Q2
21. P–B5!	. . .

The Knight is secured, QB4 is made available, and the QNP is fixed.

21. . . .	K–N1
22. N–B4	. . .

Threatening both 23. RxR and 23. P–B3.

22. . . .	KR–Q1?

A tough decision: to lose a pawn or adopt a totally defensive position (22. . . . R–K2). But a pawn is a pawn!

23. RxR	RxR
24. P–B3	N–R3

If 24. . . . N–B3 25. R–K2 R–K2 26. R–Q2 R–Q2 27. RxR NxR 28. P–QN4 and White wins the QNP with 29. N–R5.

25. NxP!	. . .

Too slow is 25. R–K2? P–B3.

25. . . .	R–Q7
26. N–B4	R–QB7
27. P–QN3	RxP
28. R–Q1!	. . .

Possession of the only open file is worth a pawn.

28. . . .	P–R4
29. R–Q8ch	K–N2
30. R–QR8	P–R5

If 30. . . . R–R8ch 31. K–B2 R–QN8 32. NxP wins.

31. RxP	RxR
32. PxR	N–N1
33. N–Q6	K–B3

Now the King and Knight make a futile effort to catch the soon-to-be-passed QRP.

34. NxNP	K–K4
35. P–R5	N–K2
36. N–Q6!	. . .

Again Q6! (to prevent 36. . . . N–B1).

| 36. . . . | K–Q5 |
| 37. P–R6 | Resigns |

For if 37. . . . KxP 38. P–R7 and the pawn queens. Instructive Knight play.

Watch the Black Knights get to work!
—Marshall

After 34. NPxP

Vidmar-Marshall, New York 1927.

| 34. . . . | N–K4! |

The Knights begin to exploit the weak squares in White's position.

| 35. B–K2 | . . . |

Of course not 35. QxR?? N–B6ch 36. K–B2 NxQ winning.

35. . . .	RxRch
36. RxR	R–Q1
37. RxRch	QxR
38. P–B6	N/2–B3
39. PxPch	KxP
40. K–N2	. . .

After 40. N–Q3 NxN 41. Q–N3ch K–R2 42. BxN Q–Q5ch 43. K–B1 N–K4 44. B–B2 Q–N7 Black has the much better ending.

| 40. . . . | N–N3 |
| 41. K–R3 | . . . |

If 41. P–R5 Q–N4ch 42. K–B1 N–B5 wins a pawn.

| 41. . . . | Q–Q3! |

Threatening to win a piece with 42. . . . N–B5ch.

| 42. K–N2 | N–Q5 |
| 43. N–N7 | . . . |

If 43. N–Q3 NxB 44. QxN QxN! 45. QxQ N–B5ch 46. K–B3 NxQ wins.

| 43. . . . | Q–K4 |
| 44. K–B1 | N–B5 |

Not 44. . . . QxP?? 44. QxPch KxQ 45. N–Q6ch K–K3 46. NxQ NxP and Black is a pawn ahead but with the win gravely in doubt!

| 45. Q–N3ch | K–R2 |
| 46. B–Q3 | N/Q–K3! |

Threatening 47. . . . Q–R8ch 48. K–B2 Q–N7ch winning the Knight.

47. B–R6	Q–R8ch
48. Q–K1	Q–N7
49. Q–K3	. . .

Black wins a piece on 49. Q–B2 Q–B8ch 50. Q–K1 Q–B3.

| 49. . . . | Q–N7ch |
| 50. K–K1 | Q–B7 |

Threatening both 51. . . . N–N7ch and 51. . . . Q–B3.

| 51. Q–KB3 | N–N7ch |
| 52. K–B1 | N/3–B5! |

Threatening 53. . . . Q–B8ch 54. K–B2 Q–K8 mate.

53. K–N1	NxP
54. Q–B1	QxP
55. N–B5	Q–K6ch
56. K–R1	QxN
57. B–Q3ch	. . .

If 57. QxN Q–Q4ch and Black mates in two.

| 57. . . . | P–B4! |
| Resigns | |

Since 58. QxN Q–Q4ch still wins for Black.

Why are some Knights different from all other Knights?

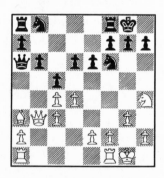

After 14. Q–N3

Mattison–Nimzovich, Carlsbad 1929.

| 14. . . . | N–B3 |

The beginning of a successful mission.

| 15. KR–Q1 | N–QR4 |
| 16. Q–N5 | . . . |

Else the foremost QBP falls.

| 16. . . . | QxQ |
| 17. PxQ | N–B5! |

An ideal post for the Knight.

| 18. B–B1 | P–QR3! |

Forcing open the QR-file in order that the Rooks may aid the Knight.

19. NPxP	RxP
20. PxP	NPxP
21. N–N2	. . .

What a difference in Knights!

| 21. . . . | N–Q4! |

One was not bad enough!

| 22. R–Q3 | KR–R1 |
| 23. P–K4 | . . . |

The QRP is indefensible.

| 23. . . . | N–K4! |
| **Resigns** | |

A prohibitive material loss is inevitable. A further continuation might produce 24. R–Q1 (24. R–Q2? N–B6ch wins) NxP 25. R–B1 (otherwise the Exchange is lost) RxP 26. RxR N–B6ch 27. K–R1 RxR with a third White pawn about to go.

Black brings about the decision by first tying white's pieces down to watch the Queenside pawns and then securing a winning superiority on the other wing.

—**Fine**

Black to move

Reshevsky–Rellstab, Kemeri 1937.

| 1. . . . | K–N3 |

The King heads for the Kingside and the Knight for the Queenside.

2. N–Q2	N–B4
3. K–Q4	N–N2
4. K–Q5	K–N4
5. K–B6	N–Q1ch
6. K–Q7	K–R5!!

A Knight for time. Black's plan is to obtain a passed pawn on both Rook files.

7. KxN	KxP
8. K–K7	P–R4
9. K–B7	P–KR5
10. KxP	K–N6

More precise is 10. . . . K–N7.

11. K–B6 . . .

Or 11. N–K4ch KxP 12. N–N5ch K–N7 13. K–B6 P–R5! 14. PxP P–N6 and Black queens the NP or RP.

11. . . .	P–R6
12. N–B1ch	K–B7
13. N–R2	P–R5!
14. PxP	P–N6
15. P–B4	P–N7
Resigns	

The Black Knight served its purpose.

A pure Knight endgame.

—Mednis

After White's 34th

Tarjan–Torre, Cleveland 1975.

34. . . . K–Q4!

A more active King and the better Knight position give Black the better chances.

35. K–K3 . . .

After 35. N–Q3?! K–Q5 36. NxN PxN! 37. K–Q2 P–QR4, Black wins the King-and-pawn ending.

| 35. . . . | P–B4 |
| 36. P–N3 | N–B3! |

To free the KP.

| 37. P–KR4? | . . . |

White should draw with 37. N–Q3.

| 37. . . . | P–B5ch! |
| 38. K–B2 | . . . |

If 38. PxP? PxP and Black's two passed KRPs are decisive.

38. . . .	PxPch
39. KxP	PxPch
40. KxP	K–Q5!

The Black King is beautifully centralized, the White one far afield. Now the main threat is 41. . . . K–K6 and 42. . . . K–Q7 winning the Knight.

41. N–K2ch	K–K6
42. N–B3	KxP
43. P–R3	. . .

The only chance.

43. . . .	P–K4!
44. P–N4	P–K5
45. P–N5	PxP
46. NxNP	P–K6
47. N–B3	N–K2!!

The type of a move that makes players Knight lovers. There is no answer.

| 48. N–N5 | . . . |

If 48. K–N5 N–Q4! 49. N–N5 (49. NxN P–K7 wins) K–K5! 50. N–Q6ch K–Q6 51. N–B5 P–K7 52. N–N3 P–K8=Q wins.

48. . . .   **N–B4ch!**
    Resigns

Pointless is 49. K–N5 P–K7 because 50. N–Q4ch has been prevented.

A Bishop can capture pawns only when they are on his color; a Knight can snare them anywhere.
                                                    —Fine

After Black's 26th

Commons–Peters, Cleveland 1975.

    27. N–K4!   . . .

Double attack. Not 27. N–QR4? B–B1! and Black holds everything.

    27. . . .   **N–K3**

Similar play to the game variation follows 27. . . . N–N2.

    28. P–KN4!   . . .

Discouraging, if not preventing, 28. . . . P–B4 and thus tying the Bishop to the defense of the KBP/3.

    28. . . .   **K–B1**

Since 28. . . . P–B4 29. PxP PxP 30. N–Q6 followed by 31. N–K1, 32. N–Q3, and 33. K–B3 soon wins the foremost doubled pawn.

29. N–K1   **. . .**

Threatening to win the QBP with 30. N–Q3.

29. . . .   **P–KR4**

Black does not care to "just sit there." With 29. . . . P–B4 30. PxP PxP 31. N–Q6 P–B5 loss of a pawn is but slightly delayed.

30. PxP!   **P–B4**

If 30. . . . PxP 31. N–Q3 wins.

31. N–Q6   **N–B5ch**

On 31. . . . K–K2 32. N–N7 PxP 33. N–Q3 B–Q5 the QBP falls to 34. P–K3.

32. K–B3   **NxRP**
33. N–Q3   **P–N4?**

If 33. . . . K–K2 34. N–N7. Everything loses.

34. NxKBP/5   **Resigns**

The Knights gallop out of the opening, romp through the middlegame, win back the Exchange, rout the King, and, with some help from the Queen, top it off with a mate.

After 16. . . . PxP

Polugaevsky–Gheorghiu, Palma de Majorca 1972.

17. N–Q5	**B–Q1**
18. R–K4ch!	**K–B2**

If 18. . . . K–B1 19. N–B4 Q–QB2 20. R–K6! and White has a clear advantage.

19. Q–N3	**N–Q5**

If 19. . . . K–B1 20. Q–N5!

20. RxN!	**PxR**
21. N–N4!	**. . .**

Threatening 22. N–K5ch.

21. . . .	**K–N3**
22. N–B6	**Q–B2**

Not 22. . . . R–N2?? 23. N/4–K5ch PxN 23. NxPch winning the Queen.

23. NxR	QxN/N
24. Q–N5	Q–B2
25. Q–Q5	R–K1

If 25. . . . B–K2 26. B–B3! Q–B4 27. NxP QxN?? 28. Q–R5 mate!

26. N–Q6	R–K4
27. B–K4ch	K–R4
28. Q–N8!	P–B4

If 28. . . . QxN?? 29. QxPch K–N5 30. Q–R4 mate.

| 29. N–B7 | . . . |

Threatening mate again.

29. . . .	PxB
30. QxPch	K–N5
31. R–KB1!	. . .

Menacing 32. R–B4 mate.

| 31. . . . | R–KB4 |
| 32. Q–N6ch | R–N4 |

Or 32. . . . B–N4 33. RxR Q–B8ch 34. K–N2 threatening 35. P–R3 mate.

33. QxPch	K–R4
34. Q–R7ch	K–N5
35. Q–R4 mate	

A Knightmare game.

—Helms

After 20. . . . Q–B2

Marchand–Collins, Cazenovia 1937.

21. N–N3 . . .

The threat of 22. N/4xP surfaces from a cluster of Knights.

21. . . . **KR–N1**

There is no way to save the pawn. So Black muddies the waters.

22. N/3xP **R–N4**
23. N–R3?? . . .

A fatal miscalculation brought on by the muddle of Knights.

23. . . . **QxN!**
24. NxR **QxR!**

White did not figure on this, believing 24. . . . Q–Q1 leaving Black the Exchange behind was forced.

25. P–K4 . . .

If 25. RxQ? RxRch 26. Q–K1 RxQ mate.

25. . . . **N–Q6**
26. R–B1 . . .

If 26. R–Q1 (26. RxQ allows mate again) N/4–N5 and Black remains a Knight up.

26. ...	N/4–B5
27. P–N3	QxRch!
Resigns	

Due to 28. KxQ R–R8ch 29. Q–K1 RxQ mate. A bit of luck!

Sweet Knight, thou art now one of the greatest men in the realm.

—Shakespeare

White wins

An Endgame Study composed by André Cheron, *Journal de Geneve* 1964.

1. P–N8=Nch!	...

The first of eight fantastic moves!

1. ...	RxN
2. RPxR=Nch	K–Q3
3. P–B8=Nch	K–K3
4. P–Q8=Nch	BxN
5. PxB=Nch	K–B3

| 6. P–N8=Nch | RxN |
| 7. RPxP=Nch | . . . |

An echo of the second move.

| 7. . . . | K–N3 |
| 8. P–B8=N mate! | |

Perhaps the ultimate in underpromoting to Knight!

The Pawn

"**The Pawn is the soul of the game**" said François André Danican Philidor, who was regarded as the strongest player in the latter part of the eighteenth century. And today many say it is the mind and body too. Its importance in modern master chess is well summed up by Capablanca in "**The winning of a Pawn among good players of even strength often means the winning of the game**" and by Keres, who wrote, "**The older I grow the more I value Pawns.**" A mere foot soldier during the early phase of the game, able to take only one or two steps on its first move, only one step thereafter, and able to capture only diagonally forward on adjacent squares, the pawn has one special advantage over all the other pieces—when it reaches the eighth rank it can be promoted to a Knight, Bishop, Rook, or Queen! Passed and protected, with the ending in sight, it becomes a factor of great strategical importance and the focal point around which play revolves. A thorough knowledge of pawn formations, the pawn majority, the outside passed pawn, the hanging pawns, the backward pawn, the candidate pawn, the ram pawn, the lever pawn, the isolated pawn, the doubled pawn, and the center pawns, the whole range of pawn weakness and pawn power, is needed to understand and exploit every position.

Every pawn is a potential Queen.

—Mason

After 31. . . . KxN

Pillsbury–Gunsberg, Hastings 1895.

32. P–K4! . . .

Magic! With the pawn at K6 apparently doomed, this is the best and only move!

32. . . . PxP
33. P–Q5ch! K–Q3

Of course, if 33. . . . KxP?? 34. P–K7 wins.

34. K–K3 P–N5

Black increases the tension by playing for an outside passed pawn. If 34. . . . P–B4 35. PxP P–QN5 36. P–B6 P–R5 37. P–B7 K–K2 38. P–Q6ch K–B1 39. P–Q7 K–K2 40. P–B8=Qch KxQ 41. P–Q8=Qch wins.

35. KxP P–R5
36. K–Q4 P–R4?

Black loses whatever he does, but 36. . . . K–K2 37. K–B4 P–N6 38. PxP P–R6 39. K–B3 P–B4! 40. PxP P–R4 41. P–N4! P–R7 42. K–N2 P–R8=Qch! 43. KxQ P–N5 44. P–N5 P–R5 45. P–N6 P–N6 46. PxP PxP 47. P–Q6ch! KxP 48. P–N7 K–B2 49. P–K7 P–N7 50. P–N8=Qch KxQ 51. P–K8=Qch K–B2 52. Q–N6 resists more.

| 37. PxP | P–R6 |
| 38. K–B4! | . . . |

Not 38. P–R6?? P–N6! 39. P–R7 (39. K–B3?? PxP and Black
wins) PxP 40. P–R8=Q P–R8=Qch and Black can draw.

38. . . .	P–B4
39. P–R6	P–B5
40. P–R7	Resigns

A classic King-and-pawn ending!

**It is well known that two pawns on the sixth rank
are stronger than a Rook.**

—Du Mont

Black to move

Sämisch–Teichmann, Teplitz-Schönau 1922.

| 1. . . . | P–Q6! |

Black sacrifices his Rook in order to obtain two connected
passed pawns.

| 2. PxR | . . . |

If 2. RxP RxR wins, and if 2. R–B3 P–Q7 3. R–B1 P–Q8=Q 4. RxQ RxR wins.

| 2. . . . | P–B5 |

Not 2. . . . P–Q7?? 3. R–Q3 and White wins.

3. R–B3	P–Q7
4. R–B1	P–B6
5. R–Q1	K–K2

Or 5. . . . P–B7 6. RxP P–B8=Q 7. R–Q4 Q–K6 and wins.

| 6. P–R4 | . . . |

If 6. P–Q6ch K–Q2 is simplest.

6. . . .	P–B7
7. RxP	P–B8=Q
and Black won	

After 8. P–Q6ch K–Q2 9. R–Q4 (9. R–Q5 QxPch 10. K–R1 QxRP wins) 9. . . . Q–K6, the Queen would immediately begin to remove the BP, QRP, KRP, and QP.

Deflections develop decisions!

Black to move

Pomar–Cuadras, Olot 1974.

Harking back to the breakthrough theme of a well-known, seventy-five-year-old endgame composition, Black queens a pawn by force.

> **1. . . .**   **P–B5!**

This pawn is not really blocked!

> **2. K–Q5**   **. . .**

The King is close but not quite close enough! If 2. KPxP P–R5! (threatening 3. . . . P–R6) 3. PxP P–N6 4. PxP P–K6 wins. And if 2. NPxP P–R5 and 3. . . . P–R6 wins.

> **2. . . .**   **P–R5!!**

Threatening 3. . . . P–R6.

> **3. KxP**   **. . .**

If 3. PxRP P–N6! 4. BPxP PxKP 5. KxP P–K7 and Black wins.

> **3. . . .**   **P–B6!**

Threatening to win with 4. . . . BPxP, and thus deflecting the NP/2.

> **4. PxBP**   **P–R6**
> **Resigns**

For if 5. PxP P–R7 6. K–B3 P–R8=Qch wins. Deflection plus breakthrough equals Queen.

The passed pawn is a criminal, who should be kept under lock and key; mild measures, such as police surveillance, are not sufficient.

—Nimzovich

After 19. N–K2

Jansa–Kaplan, Hastings 1976.

A complicated middlegame position. Black is a pawn ahead, but White is trying to remedy that with 19. . . . N–R3 (the only safe square for the Knight) 20. BxP.

| 19. . . . | P–Q4! |

However, Black goes his own way, banking on three passed pawns instead of his Knight.

| 20. KPxP | . . . |

Better is 20. BPxP PxP 21. P–K5 N–R3 22. QxP Q–K2 23. N–B3, although Black's two connected passed pawns constitute a clear advantage. If 20. PxN? PxKP and Black regains his piece.

| 20. . . . | PxP |
| 21. PxN | . . . |

White insists on being shown. 21. PxP is more prudent.

21. . . .	QPxP
22. B–K3	Q–Q6
23. R–K1	BPxP!

Three connected "criminals"—none of which is under lock and key!

24.	P–B5	KR–K1
25.	K–B2	Q–K5
26.	R–Q1	P–N6
27.	N–N3	Q–B7ch
28.	R–Q2	Q–B6
29.	PxP!?	. . .

White returns the piece in order to win one of the three passed pawns.

29.	. . .	RxB
30.	PxBPch	K–R1
31.	RxR	QxR/7ch
32.	N–K2	. . .

Threatening to win with 33. R–K8ch B–B1 34. RxR.

32.	. . .	R–KB1
33.	QxBP	P–N7
34.	R–Q3	. . .

If 34. Q–N3 B–Q5 wins.

34.	. . .	Q–N5!

Forcing the exchange of Queens and removing any doubts.

35.	QxQ	PxQ

Doubled and isolated, the pawns look less impressive, but they still win.

36.	R–QN3	RxPch
37.	K–K1	B–B6ch
38.	NxB	. . .

Or 38. K–Q1 R–Q2ch 39. K–B2 R–Q7ch 40. K–N1 RxN wins.

38.	. . .	PxN

Undoubled and reunited again.

39. K–Q1	R–B8ch
Resigns	

Since 40. K–B2 R–B8ch 41. K–Q3 P–N8=Qch 42. RxQ RxR 43. KxP R–N8 wins. All the "criminals" were liquidated, but they were succeeded by an archfiend—the Rook!

A pawn majority on one wing can be of more value than a single passed pawn, provided that the foremost pawn is sufficiently advanced.

—Du Mont

Black to move

Grigoriev–Subarev, U.S.S.R. 1926.

1. . . .	P–N4!

Menacing 2. . . . PxP 3. PxP P–B5 4. P–B4 P–Q6 and wins.

2. PxPch	K–N3!

Foresight.

3. K–K6	P–R5

Seeking 4. . . . P–R6.

4. PxP	. . .

It is not check, and it does not win a tempo, as it would have if Black had played 2. . . . KxP?

4. . . .	P–B5
5. P–B4	P–Q6

and Black won

The runoff could be 6. PxP PxP 7. P–B5 P–Q7 8. P–B6 P–Q8=Q 9. P–B7 Q–Q1 10. K–B5 K–B4 11. K–N6 K–Q3 12. K–N7 K–K2 13. P–N6 Q–B1ch 14. K–N6 QxPch with an elementary win.

A passed pawn increases in strength as the number of pieces on the board diminishes.
—Capablanca

After Black's 45th

A. Cheklov–O. Batakov, Riga 1974.

    46. P–K6!!   . . .

A surprise move, a sacrifice based on the power of the passed pawn.

    46. . . .   R–K1

If 46. . . . BxB? 47. P–K7 R–K1 48. R–B8! wins.

47. P–K7! . . .

Offering both the Bishop and the KP.

47. . . . **N–B4**

If 47. . . . BxB 48. R–B8 wins. And if 47. . . . RxP 48. R–B8ch R–K1 49. RxR mate!

48. R–B2! . . .

Threatening 49. R–B8ch RxR 50. PxR=Q mate!

48. . . . **K–N1**
49. BxN **PxB**
50. B–K6ch **K–R1**
51. R–B7! **Resigns**

52. B–Q7 wins the Rook (51. . . . B–B3 52. R–B8ch RxR 53. PxR=Q mate). A star passed pawn with a great supporting cast.

Pure pawn endings are the easiest endings to win.

—Fine

White to move

An Endgame Study. Author unknown.

1. P–K4!   . . .

With the winning idea of 2. P–K5 PxP 3. P–N5 PxP 4. PxP K–B3
5. P–B6 PxP 6. P–N6.

1. . . .   **K–B3**

Threatening 2. . . . K–Q3 to win with his outside passed pawn.

2. P–K5!   **PxP**

3. P–K6 must be prevented.

3. P–N5   **PxP?**

A prolongation is 3. . . . K–Q3! 4. P–B6 K–K3 5. PxNP K–B2 6.
PxP P–N4! 7. K–K4! P–N5 8. K–Q3!! K–N1 9. K–B4 P–K5 10. KxP
P–K6 11. K–B3 P–K7 12. K–Q2 K–B2 13. KxP K–N1 14. K–B3
K–B2 15. K–B4 K–N1 16. K–B5 K–B2 16. P–R5 K–N1 17. K–B6
K–R2 18. K–B7 and White wins.

4. P–B6!   **Resigns**

After 4. . . . PxBP (forced) 5. P–R5!, the sole remaining White
pawn queens and wins the game.

Two lowly little Rook pawns, doubled and isolated, are able to thwart His Imperial Majesty.

Black to move

An Endgame Study. Author unknown.

| 1. . . . | P–R5! |

Black is a pawn behind, but, because of the peculiar placement of the pawns and the offside White King, he has a won game. The threat is 2. . . . P–N5! 3. PxP P–R6 winning the race to queen.

| 2. K–K4 | . . . |

This is the only hope.

| 2. . . . | P–N5! |

Threatening 3. . . . PxP 4. KxP P–R7 5. K–B3 P–R8=Qch and wins.

| 3. KxP | PxP |
| 4. K–B3 | . . . |

Just in time to stop 4. . . . P–R7.

| 4. . . . | K–N4 |
| 5. P–Q4 | . . . |

If 5. K any P–R7 wins.

| 5. . . . | KxP |
| **Resigns** | |

Zugzwang! Again, if 6. K any P–R7 wins. Or if 6. P–Q5 K–B4 7. K–B4 P–R7 8. K–B5 P–R8=Q 9. P–B4 Q–B6 and wins.

An outside passed pawn spreads fear in the enemy camp.

White to move

An Endgame Study by A. Troitski 1913.

        1. P–KB6!   . . .

Fatally premature is 1. P–R4?? PxP e.p. 2. PxP K–N6!! and Black mates with his RP in four or five moves.

        1. . . .   **PxP**
        2. KxP   . . .

2. P–R4?? loses as in the preceding note.

        2. . . .   **K–N4**

The run for the RP is off.

        3. P–R4   **PxP e.p.**
        4. PxP   **K–B4**
        5. P–R4   **K–K4**

By threatening to win all White's pawns, this almost turns the tables, but . . .

        6. P–Q6!   . . .

. . . this keeps them from turning. Curiously, 6. P–B6 wins slightly faster than Troitski's solution: 6. . . . PxP 7. P–R5.

| 6. . . . | PxP |

Or 6. . . . P–B3 7. P–R5 K–Q4 8. P–R6 KxP 9. P–R7 and Black cannot catch the runaway.

| 7. P–B6! | . . . |

Very clever! Black is forced into a self-block.

| 7. . . . | PxP |
| 8. P–R5 | Resigns |

Since 8. . . . K–Q4 9. P–R6 K–B4 10. P–R7 K–N3 11. P–R8=Q resolves all doubt. Without either the QBP or the QP Black would catch the pawn!

A forced mate in seven, White has no other method of winning.

—Tattersall

White wins

An Endgame Study. Author unknown.

| 1. P–R5! | . . . |

Depriving Black of one of his two tempos and thus forcing his reply.

| 1. . . . | P–R6 |
| 2. P–N4ch | . . . |

2. P–N3 stalemate!

| 2. . . . | K–R5 |
| 3. P–R3! | . . . |

Tempo!

| 3. . . . | P–R4 |
| 4. P–N5! | . . . |

Not 4. PxP?? KxP 5. KxP?? K–N5 and Black wins.

| 4. . . . | PxP |
| 5. P–R4 | . . . |

Tempo!

5. . . .	P–N5
6. K–B4	P–N6
7. PxP mate!	

Predestined pawns! This is the original version of several subsequent similar studies.

The Endgame

The Endgame is the North Star by which a course may be set in both the Opening and the Middlegame. In such major Openings as the Benoni Defense (Accelerated Variation), the Queen's Gambit Declined (Orthodox Defense), and the Ruy Lopez (Exchange Variation), Pawn formations are established as early as the 5th, 13th, and the 4th moves, respectively, formations that determine play in the Ending. In the Benoni and QGD, Black inherits a Queenside Pawn majority to exploit, and in the Ruy, White has a healthy Kingside Pawn majority against Black's unhealthy Queenside Pawns (the classic example being Lasker–Capablanca, St. Petersburg, 1914). And underlying much of the complicated tactics and positional maneuvering of the Middlegame is the everpresent question of whether or not to make a transition Endgame: whether a win can be had there based on material advantage, superior Pawn structure, or better piece play, or whether an unfavorable Middlegame makes it imperative! The answer lies only in knowledge of the characteristics and requirements of Endgame play.

But that knowledge and understanding is all too often limited or lacking, especially among students and intermediate players, due to the comparatively few books on the subject and the aversion of many to studying it. This in the face of Chernev's dictum: **"If you want to win at Chess, begin with the Ending"**; and Mason's barbed inquiry: **"A player in a fog as to the movements of two or three pieces—what will he do with two-and-thirty?"**

The superiority of the Bishop over the Knight is most evident when there are pawns on both sides of the board.

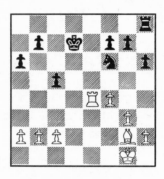

After 23. . . . KxQ

Fischer–Taimanov, Vancouver 1971.

24.	R–K5	P–QN3
25.	B–B1	P–QR4
26.	B–B4	. . .

With his last three moves White has improved the position of his pieces, saddled Black with a weak-color complex, and forced the enemy Rook to assume a defensive stance.

26.	. . .	R–KB1
27.	K–N2	K–Q3

If 27. . . . N–K1 28. B–N5ch K–Q1 29. R–Q5ch K–B1 30. R–Q7 N–B2 31. B–B6 and Black is close to zugzwang.

28.	K–B3	N–Q2
29.	R–K3	N–N1
30.	R–Q3ch	K–B2
31.	P–B3!	. . .

Now the Knight cannot hope to occupy its Q5.

31.	. . .	N–B3
32.	R–K3	K–Q3

33. P–QR4	N–K2
34. P–R3	N–B3
35. P–R4	. . .

With the prospect of 36. P–KN4 and 37. P–N5.

35. . . .	P–R4
36. R–Q3ch	K–B2
37. R–Q5	P–B4

If 37. . . . P–N3? 38. B–N5 followed by 39. P–B5 cracking the Kingside.

38. R–Q2	R–B3
39. R–K2	K–Q2
40. R–K3	P–N3
41. B–N5	R–Q3
42. K–K2	K–Q1
43. R–Q3	. . .

With the White King able to reach QN5 and the Black Kingside Pawns fixed on white squares, the time has come to exchange Rooks and demonstrate the Bishop's superiority.

43. . . .	K–B2
44. RxR	KxR
45. K–Q3!	. . .

Threatening 46. BxN KxB 47. K–B4 K–Q3 48. K–N5 and wins.

45. . . .	N–K2
46. B–K8	K–Q4
47. B–B7ch	K–Q3
48. K–B4	K–B3
49. B–K8ch	K–N2
50. K–N5	N–B1
51. B–B6ch	. . .

No jokes. If 51. BxP??? N–Q3 mate!

| 51. . . . | K–B2 |
| 52. B–Q5 | N–K2 |

| 53. B–B7 | K–N2 |
| 54. B–N3! | . . . |

The Bishop is headed for an even better diagonal.

54. . . .	K–R2
55. B–Q1	K–N2
56. B–B3ch	K–B2

Or 56. . . . K–R2 57. B–N2 and Black is in zugzwang.

57. K–R6	N–N1
58. B–Q5	N–K2
59. B–B4	K–B3
60. B–B7	K–B2
61. B–K8	K–Q1
62. BxP!!	. . .

Strategy and tactics, all planned and calculated. The two connected passed Pawns White obtains are soon decisive.

62. . . .	NxB
63. KxP	K–Q2
64. KxBP	N–K2
65. P–QN4	PxP
66. PxP	N–B1
67. P–R5	N–Q3
68. P–N5	N–K5ch
69. K–N6	K–B1

If 69. . . . NxP 70. P–R6 K–B1 71. P–R7 wins.

| 70. K–B6 | K–N1 |
| 71. P–N6 | Resigns |

A very instructive Ending.

An inelastic pawn structure is an esthetic eyesore.

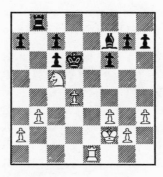

After 31. . . . B–B2

Lasker–Steinitz, Moscow 1896/97.

32. N–K4ch!		K–Q2

Not 32. . . . K–Q4 33. K–K3 with 34. R–QB1 looming.

33. K–K3	B–Q4
34. N–B5ch	. . .

The beautiful Knight must not be traded.

34. . . .	K–Q3
35. K–Q3	P–KR4
36. P–KR4	R–KR1
37. K–B3	R–QN1
38. P–B4	R–N1

White obtains a decisive advantage on 38. . . . BxKNP 39. R–K6ch K–Q4 40. R–K7.

39. P–N3	P–N4

Like the 35th move, this weakens the Kingside.

40. BPxP	PxP
41. R–K5	PxP

| 42. PxP | R–N6ch |
| 43. K–N4 | R–N5 |

Counterplay, but not of a serious nature. If 43. . . . B–B2 44. RxP! BxR 45. N–K4ch K–Q4 46. NxR wins.

44. N–N7ch	K–Q2
45. RxP	RxPch
46. K–R5	B–B2
47. R–R6!	R–Q7
48. N–B5ch	K–K2
49. P–R4	R–Q3
50. R–R8	R–Q4
51. P–N4	B–K1

Preventing 52. R–R8. If 51. . . . R–Q1 52. RxR KxR 53. K–R6 with an easy win for White.

52. R–R6	R–B4
53. R–K6ch	K–Q1
54. R–K4!	B–B2
55. K–R6	B–Q4
56. R–Q4	K–B1
57. KxP	R–R4
58. R–KB4	R–R1
59. P–KR5	B–R7

Or 59. . . . K–Q1 60. K–N7 RxP 61. P–R5 and the passed pawn marches right in.

60. P–R6	B–Q4
61. P–R7	B–R7
62. R–K4	B–B2
63. R–R4	B–R7

If 63. . . . B–N3 64. R–R6 BxP 65. P–R5 K–Q1 66. K–N7 wins.

64. N–K4	B–N6
65. P–R5	B–B7
66. R–N4!	Resigns

The threat of 67. R–N8ch is too much. If 66. . . . RxP 67. R–N8ch
K–Q2 68. N–B6ch wins the Exchange. And if 66. . . . B–N6 67.
N–B6 (threatening 68. R–N8ch) wins. A great Endgame.

**The theory of the ending proper is concerned to
a large extent with the conversion of an advantage
of one pawn into a win.**

—Fine

After 24. R–Q1

Dvoretsky–Tal, U.S.S.R. 1976.

| | 24. . . . | Q–B4! |

A double attack on the Knight and QP.

25. N–N4	RxP
26. RxR	QxR
27. P–KN3	. . .

If 27. NxP B–B5 28. N–N4 P–KR4 29. N–B2 (29. P–KN3 PxN
30. PxB PxP wins) 29. . . . BxP and Black can convert successfully.

27. . . .	P–B3
28. K–B2	P–KR4
29. N–B2	K–B1

As usual, the King must assume an active role in the Ending.

30. N–K4	B–R3
31. P–KN4	P–R5!
32. P–KR3	K–K2
33. P–N3	P–N3
34. PxP	PxP
35. Q–Q1	. . .

This makes it rather easy for Black, but if 35. Q–B2 Q–Q6ch 36. K–N2 B–K6 37. QxP Q–K7ch 38. K–R3 B–B8ch 39. K–N4 Q–N7ch 40. K–B5 Q–N4 mates!

35. . . .	QxQch
36. KxQ	P–R4
37. K–K2	. . .

If 37. N–B5 B–K6 38. N–N7 B–N3! traps the Knight.

37. . . .	K–K3
38. P–R4	. . .

Now threatening to win the QRP with 39. N–B5ch and 40. N–N7.

38. . . .	B–B1
39. P–N5	P–B4
40. N–Q2	K–Q4

Readying 41. . . . B–K2 and 42. . . . BxP.

41. P–B4	PxP
Resigns	

On 42. K–B3 B–R6! 43. KxP (43. N–N1 B–B8) B–B8 44. K–K3 P–B5ch 45. K–K2 BxN 46. KxB K–K5 wins.

A remarkable zugzwang position: a tempo-gaining series of moves is repeated four times!
—Marshall

After 40. P–R3

Teichmann–Marshall, San Sebastian 1911.

40. . . .	R–B8ch
41. K–N2	R–N8
42. B–Q1	R–K8!
43. B–K2	. . .

Practically forced. On 43. B–B2 (43. K–B3 R–K6ch 44. K–N2 R–Q6 45. RxR BxR and Black wins the KNP or KRP) 43. . . . BxB 44. KxB P–R5 45. K–N2 PxP 46. KxP R–K6ch 47. K–N2 P–R4 48. R–QB2 K–Q5 49. R–Q2ch K–K4 and the Black King penetrates victoriously.

43. . . .	P–R4!
44. K–B3	R–B8ch
45. K–N2	R–N8
46. B–Q1	R–K8!
47. B–K2	P–KR5!

Immobilizing the White Kingside pawns.

| 48. K–B3 | R–B8ch |
| 49. K–N2 | R–N8 |

| 50. B–Q1 | R–K8! |
| 51. B–K2 | P–KB3! |

Another tempo!

52. K–B3	R–B8ch
53. K–N2	R–N8
54. B–Q1	R–K8!
55. B–K2	P–B3
56. K–B3	R–B8ch
57. K–N2	R–N8ch
58. K–B3	P–N4!

Menacing 59. . . . P–N5ch 60. PxP PxP mate.

59. P–N4ch	PxPch
60. PxPch	RxP
61. QPxP	PxP

Menacing 62. . . . R–N6 mate.

| 62. R–Q5ch | . . . |

If 62. R–R2 R–N6ch 63. K–Q2 P–B6ch wins.

62. . . .	KxP!
63. RxPch	KxR
64. KxR	K–K4

Heading for KN6—as presaged by 47. . . . P–KR5.

65. KxP	B–B2ch
66. K–Q3	K–B5
67. B–B1	K–N6
68. K–K3	B–Q4
69. K–K2	P–B4
70. K–K3	B–K3
71. K–K2	P–N5!

A lethal lever. Black will win with his RP.

| 72. RPxP | . . . |

The alternative likewise loses: 72. BPxP PxP 73. K–K3 B–Q2 74. K–K2 B–N4ch! 75. K–K1 B–B3 76. PxP BxP 77. BxB KxB 78. P–N5 P–R6 79. P–N6 P–R7 80. P–N7 P–R8=Qch 81. K–K2 Q–R2.

72. . . .	PxP
73. K–K3	B–Q2
74. PxP	. . .

Or 74. P–B4 K–R7 75. K–B2 P–N6ch 76. K–K1 B–N5 wins. Or 74. K–K2 B–N4ch 75. K–K1 B–B3 76. PxP BxP wins.

74. . . .	BxP
75. K–K4	B–B1
76. K–K3	B–Q2
Resigns	

Since after 77. K–K2 B–B3 78. K–K1 BxP 79. B–N5 P–R6 settles matters.

Two advantages—the better King position and a good Bishop against a bad Bishop
—total a won game.

After 38. . . . K–B1

Brown–Grefe, Oberlin 1975.

39. RPxP	. . .

White sets up a third Pawn target.

39. . . .	**RPxP**
40. PxP	**PxP**
41. B–B3	. . .

The beginning of a Bishop maneuver which enables the King to reach KN4.

41. . . .	**B–K3**
42. B–K2	**B–Q2**
43. B–B3	**B–K3**
44. B–K2	**B–Q2**
45. B–N4!	**B–B3**

Black cannot afford the luxury of trading Bishops.

46. B–B8	. . .

Threatening to win with 47. K–N4 and 48. KxP.

46. . . .	**K–N2**
47. K–N4	**K–N3**
48. P–N3	**K–B3**

Black must admit the White King. If 48. . . . B–K1 49. B–N7 B–Q2ch 50. K–B3 B–K3 51. B–B6 and the QNP falls.

49. K–R5	. . .

Destination Q8.

49. . . .	**B–K1ch**
50. K–R6	. . .

Threatening 51. B–N7 B–B2 52. B–B6.

50. . . .	**B–B3**
51. K–R7	**B–K1**
52. B–N4	**B–N3ch**

Or 52. . . . K–B2 (52. . . . K–K2 53. K–N7) 53. B–R5ch K–K2 54. BxB KxB 55. K–N6 and White wins.

53. K–N8	B–B4
54. B–K2	B–Q2
55. K–B8	P–N5

If 55. . . . B–B3 56. B–N4 and White gets to K8 or K7 with his King.

56. B–B1	B–B3
57. B–N2	B–N2
58. K–K8	K–K3
59. K–Q8	K–Q3
60. B–B1	B–B3
61. B–Q3!	Resigns

Realistic. After 61. . . . B–Q2 (to prevent 62. B–B5 and 63. BxP) 62. B–K2! K–B3 (62. . . . K–K3 63. BxPch K–Q3 64. B–K2! wins) 63. BxPch KxB (63. . . . K–Q3 64. B–K2!) 64. KxB KxP 65. K–Q6 K–B5 66. K–K5 K–Q6 67. KxP and White queens (promotes!) first.

Three advantages—better King position, aggressive Rook against a passive Rook, and two lively Knights opposed by two dead Bishops
—total a won game.

After 32. R–Q2

Vukcevich–Lombardy, Oberlin 1975.

| 32. . . . | **P–N5!** |

In order to handicap White with two isolated pawns.

| 33. **K–B2** | **R–B1!** |

There are greener pastures for the Rook on the other side.

34. **K–K3**	**PxP**
35. **KxP**	**R–KR1**
36. **R–KB2**	**R–R3**

Threatening 37. . . . R–B3ch 38. K–K3 RxR 39. KxR NxPch.

| 37. **K–K3** | **R–N3** |
| 38. **R–K2?** | . . . |

Better is 38. R–R2, and if 38. . . . R–N5 39. R–R4.

| 38. . . . | **N–B5ch** |
| 39. **K–B3** | **R–B3ch** |

Another way is 39. . . . N–Q6 40. P–N3 PxP 41. PxP NxBch 42. RxN N–Q7ch 43. K–B2 NxNP.

40. K–N2	N–Q6

Wild horses! Threat: 41. . . . NxBch 42. RxN NxP.

41. P–N3	N–R4!
42. PxP	. . .

If 42. P–QN4 N–B5 and the Knights exert a terrific bind.

42. . . .	N–B5!

Back at the old post. White is in zugzwang.

43. K–N1	R–B6
44. P–N4	NxB!

Harvest time.

45. RxN	N–Q7
46. B–N2	RxP
47. R–Q1	R–B7!
48. P–R3	K–B3

To tip the scales with the added weight of the King.

49. R–K1	K–N4
50. R–K3	R–B5

Embarrassment of riches.

51. P–R5	KxP
52. K–R2	K–B5
53. R–Q3	R–Q5!
54. R–B3	R–B5
55. R–Q3	R–Q5
56. R–B3	P–B3

With the time pressure solved, Black goes about wrapping it up.

57. R–B7	. . .

Too late, the Rook becomes active.

57. . . .	N–B6ch
58. K–R3	. . .

If 58. BxN KxB 59. RxP KxP wins going away.

58.	. . .	R–Q6!
59.	RxP	RxP
60.	R–Q7	N–K8ch
61.	K–R2	R–R7
62.	RxP	. . .

Or 62. R–KN7 NxB 63. RxN RxP 64. R–B2ch KxP and wins.

62.	. . .	RxBch
63.	K–R1	R–R7
64.	RxPch	KxP
65.	P–R6	N–B6
66.	R–R6	K–K6
	Resigns	

In light of 67. P–R7 R–R8ch 68. K–N2 R–N8ch 69. K–R3 K–B7
70. R–KN6 RxR 71. P–R8=Q R–N6 mate.

Gaining the Exchange is one thing, making it pay off another.

White to move

Hort–Hulak, Vinkovci 1976.

1. K–Q4   . . .

The King must help. Threat: 2. P–K5.

1. . . .   **N–Q2**

Or 1. . . . P–B3 2. N–B4 N–N4 3. NxP! KxN 4. R–N6ch K–K2 5. KxN NxPch 6. K–B6 N–Q3 7. R–R6 N–B1 8. K–B7 and White wins.

2. R–N7!   . . .

A mistake is 2. N–B4? N–N4 3. K–K3 N–B4! 4. P–K5 PxP 5. NxP K–Q3 6. K–Q4 N/B–K3ch 7. PxN NxPch 8. K–K4 P–B4ch and White must fight for a draw.

2. . . .   **N–N4**
3. K–K3!   **N–R2**

Or 3. . . . P–B3 4. N–B4 N–B2 5. N–N6 N–K4 6. N–B8ch K–Q1 7. NxP and White wins.

4. N–B4   **N–B3**
5. K–Q4   **P–N4**

Black is running out of moves.

6. R–R7   **P–N5**
7. N–K3   **Resigns**

There is no defense to 8. N–B5ch 9. NxQP, and the advance of the White pawns.

Tie up your opponent on one side and then break through on the other side.

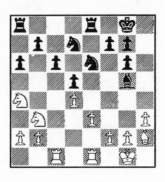

After 20, . . . N–K3

Rubinstein–Takacs, Budapest 1926.

| 21. N–R5! | R–R2 |

A horrid-looking move, but if 21. . . . N–Q1 22. B–B7 R–R2 (anyway) 23. N–B5 NxN 24. PxN (threatening 25. B–N6) with a winning position for White.

| 22. K–B1! | B–Q1 |
| 23. P–QN4! | P–KB4 |

If 23. . . . B–B2 24. BxB NxB 25. N–B5 NxN 26. NPxN and White operates on the QN-file as in the actual game.

24. N–N2!	P–KN4
25. N–Q3	K–B2
26. R–B2	B–N3
27. B–Q6!	N–Q1
28. N–B5!	NxN
29. BxN	BxB
30. NPxB	. . .

The QN-file is opened in order to exert the utmost pressure on the backward QNP.

30. . . .	K–K2
31. R–N2	K–Q2
32. KR–N1	K–B1
33. K–K2	R–K2
34. K–B3	R–K5
35. P–N4!	. . .

With all but one of the Black pieces tied down to the defense of the QNP, White breaks decisively on the opposite wing.

| 35. . . . | P–KN3 |

If 35. . . . P–B5 36. N–B4! wins.

| 36. R–N1 | N–B2 |
| 37. P–KR4! | NPxP |

Or 37. . . . RxNP 38. RxR PxRch 39. KxP PxP 40. KxP K–B2 41. R–N1 K–B1 42. R–N1 P–N4ch 43. K–R5 K–Q2 44. K–N6 K–K2 45. R–KR1 (or back to the Queenside with 45. R–QN1!) and White wins.

| 38. PxP | PxP |

If 38. . . . P–KN4 39. N–B4! is the trick.

39. R–N7	N–Q1
40. R–N8	P–B5
41. R–R8!	PxP
42. PxP	K–Q2
43. R–N2!	. . .

Threatening 44. R/2–N8.

43. . . .	R–K1
44. RxP	R–K2
45. R–R8	K–B2
46. R/2–N8	R–Q2
47. N–N3!	P–R4
48. N–B1	R–R1
49. N–Q3	. . .

Planning to penetrate with 50. N–K5 or 50. N–B4 and 51. N–K6 (with any necessary preparation) and thus forcing a desperate response.

49. . . .		P–N4
50.	PxP e.p.ch	KxP
51.	N–B5	R–Q3
52.	P–R4	R–B1
53.	K–N4!	Resigns

There is no defense to the coming invasion of the White King. For example, 53. . . . R–R1 (53. . . . R–N1 54. R–N7! threatening 55. RxN RxR 56. R–N7 mate) 54. K–B5 R–B1 55. R–B8 R–N1 56. K–K5 and White wins a piece. Or 53. . . . K–B2 54. R–N7ch K–N1 55. R/8–R7, and mate with 56. N–R6ch and 57. R–R7 follows.

The ending is that part of the game in which we must convert into a win any advantages won during the opening or middlegame.

—Keres

After 27. RxB

Augustin–D. Byrne, Lugano 1968.

27. . . .   N–N3

Now, inexorably, the pieces begin to find their best squares, the center pawn mass moves forward, and the opponent is battered into submission.

28.	R–N5	K–B2
29.	R–N2	P–K4!
30.	P–N4	P–B5
31.	P–Q4	P–K5
32.	N–K3	B–K3
33.	R–R2	P–QR4!

Beating him to the punch!

34.	P–QR4	. . .

If 34. PxP R–QR1.

34.	. . .	RPxP
35.	BPxP	PxP
36.	RxP	R–QN1
37.	N–B2	N–B5
38.	R–R7ch	K–N3
39.	R–R6	K–N4
40.	K–B2	P–R4
41.	K–K3	B–N5!

With the idea of 42. . . . B–Q8, 43. . . . BxN, and 44. . . . RxP.

42.	BxP?!	B–Q8!

Not 42. . . . PxB?? 43. P–R4ch K–B4 44. R–R5ch K–B3 45. KxN and White takes over.

43.	B–N3	R–QB1
44.	P–R4ch	K–N5
45.	B–R4	. . .

Or 45. K–Q2 BxN 46. BxB P–K6ch and Black wins the Bishop.

45.	. . .	R–B6ch!
46.	K–Q2	R–Q6ch
47.	K–B1	KxP
48.	P–N5	P–K6

Wins a piece by the threat of 49. . . . BxN 50. BxB P–K7.

49.	NxP	BxB
50.	N–B5ch	K–N4
51.	RxB	KxN
52.	K–B2	R–KN6
53.	P–N6	R–N1
54.	P–N7	R–N1
	Resigns	

Discovering the way to win in some endings is akin to making one's way through a mine field.

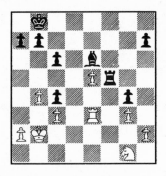

After 34. RxQ

Ruth–Collins, St. Louis 1960.

34. . . .		R–B7ch

First blood.

35. N–K2		. . .

Immediately fatal is 35. R–K2?? R–B8 36. R–N2 B–Q4.

35. . . .		RxP
36. K–R3		K–B2

37. N–B4	K–Q2
38. R–K4	. . .

Threatening to draw with 39. NxB KxN 40. RxNP.

38. . . .	B–B4!

The blockade must be lifted to secure play against the isolated King. Now, however, White gets what he has been seeking.

39. P–K6ch	K–K2
40. RxP	B–N8

The idea is 41. . . . P–N4, 42. . . . BxP, and 43. . . . B–B5 with a mating net.

41. R–Q4	BxP
42. P–B4	P–N4!

Menacing mate or the win of the Exchange with 43. . . . BxP.

43. R–Q7ch	. . .

If 43. PxP PxP 44. N–R5 BxP wins.

43. . . .	K–K1
44. N–R5	. . .

Threatening 45. N–B6ch K–B1 46. R–B7 mate. White must go into the lost Rook-and-Pawn Endgame in view of 44. RxQRP (44. PxP PxP and the mate threat with 45. . . . B–B5 and 46. . . . R–R7 arises) 44. . . . BxP 45. R–R8ch K–K2 46. R–R7ch K–B3 47. R–B7ch K–N4 48. R–N7ch K–R3 with a forced mate for Black.

44. . . .	RxN
45. KxB	PxP
46. R–QB7	R–R6
47. RxBP	RxP
48. R–B7	. . .

Or 48. RxP P–KR4 and wins.

48. . . .	P–KR4
49. R–R7	R–N6

50. RxKRP	RxP
51. R–QB5	K–K2
52. K–R3	R–N6ch
53. K–R2	KxP
54. RxP	R–N6
55. K–N2	. . .

Or 55. R–R4 K–B4 56. RxP R–QB6 and Black wins with a Lucena-like position.

55. . . .	K–B4
56. K–B2	R–K6
57. K–Q2	R–K2
58. R–B8	K–B5
Resigns	

The Middlegame

"The Middle Game is Chess in excelsis, the most beautiful part of the game, in which a lively imagination can exercise itself most fully and creatively in conjuring up magnificent combinations," wrote Tarrasch. Few chess players would take exception to this enthusiastic appraisal. For it is in this second phase of the game that the great battles of the board are fought; and it is here, according to some psychologists, that true chess genius is evident—where the emphasis is on creativity and not on memory.

Standing between the Opening and the Endgame, the Middlegame is influenced by both, inheriting the advantages and disadvantages of the former and relying on the latter to maximize the advantages and minimize the disadvantages as they have been acquired and remolded.

"The Middlegame is chess itself; Chess, with all its possibilities, its attacks, defenses, sacrifices, etc.," said Znosko-Borovsky. And, it should be added, its plans, its Pawn positions, its concepts of force, space, and time, its transitions, its mating attacks, its combinations and points of attack, its psychological tensions, and its need for clear, cold, analytical ability.

In sum, once again to quote Tarrasch: "Before the Endgame the gods have placed the Middlegame."

Each position must be regarded as a problem, where it is a question of finding the correct move, almost always only one, demanded by that position.
—Tarrasch

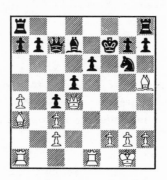

After 17. . . . K–B2

Fischer–Larsen, Denver 1971.

18. P–B4! . . .

White, having sacrificed a pawn to prevent castling, now procedes to break up the center and to open the KB-file to get at the exposed Black King.

18. . . . **KR–K1**

After 18. . . . K–N1 19. P–B5 N–B5 20. B–B3 R–K1 21. R–K5 PxP 22. QR–K1 Black has a lost position.

19. P–B5 **PxP**
20. QxQPch **K–B3**

If 20. . . . B–K3? 21. RxB RxR 22. QxPch R–B3 23. Q–Q5ch R–K3 24. R–B1ch and Black loses a Bishop.

21. B–B3 **N–K4**
22. Q–Q4! . . .

Calculating eight moves ahead! Threat: 23. B–Q6 winning.

22. . . . **K–N3**

On 22. . . . QR–Q1 23. B–Q6 Q–R4 24. B–Q5 wins the Knight.

23. RxN	QxR
24. QxB	QR–Q1

White wins the Ending with 24. . . . QxP 25. Q–Q6ch Q–B3 (25. . . . K–N4? 26. P–R4ch KxP 27. Q–B4 mate) 26. QxQch KxQ 27. BxP.

25. QxP	Q–K6ch

Critics have recommended 25. . . . QxP.

26. K–B1	R–Q7

A chilling situation, but White had foreseen it on his 22nd move! Now if 26. . . . QxP? 27. B–N2 wins.

27. Q–B6ch	R–K3
28. B–B5!	. . .

Putting the picture into focus. Not 28. Q–B5? R–B7ch 29. K–N1 RxBch and Black wins.

28. . . .	R–B7ch

Forced. If 28. . . . Q–K4 29. B–Q4 wins, and if 28. . . . RxQ 29. BxQ wins.

29. K–N1	RxNPch
30. KxR	Q–Q7ch
31. K–R1	RxQ
32. BxR	. . .

With a Rook and two Bishops for a Queen, White has a winning material advantage, but some technical problems remain.

32. . . .	QxP/6?

Best is 32. . . . P–QR4! denying White a passed QRP. Then if 33. R–N1ch K–B2 34. B–Q4 P–N4 35. B–Q5ch K–N3 36. BxP QxP/7.

33. R–N1ch	K–B3
34. BxP	P–N4

35. B–N6	QxP
36. P–R5	Q–N7
37. B–Q8ch	K–K3
38. P–R6	Q–R6
39. B–N7	Q–B4
40. R–N1	P–B6
41. B–N6	Resigns

If 41. . . . Q–R6 42. P–R7 P–B7 43. R–K1ch K–B3 44. P–R8=Q P–B8=Q 45. RxQ QxRch 46. B–N1 wins.

When we have the better development and our pieces display more activity, then these circumstances must be exploited at once.

—**Kotov**

Black to move

Veiliat–Alekhine.

| 1. . . . | Q–R6! |

White must not be given time to play 2. B–K2 and 3. O–O.

| 2. R–B2 | R–Q1 |
| 3. R–Q2 | . . . |

Not 3. Q–B1? N–N5! 4. QxQ?? NxRch 5. K–K2 NxQ and Black wins.

3. . . .	B–N5
4. B–K2	RxR
5. NxR	. . .

If 5. QxR R–Q1 and Black has a distinct advantage.

5. . . .	BxB
6. Q–R1ch	. . .

The only way to save the QRP.

6. . . .	P–B3
7. KxB	Q–R3ch
8. N–B4	P–QN4
9. N–N2	P–N5ch
10. K–K1	. . .

On 10. N–B4 N–R4 11. R–QB1 R–QB1, Black wins a pawn.

10. . . .	R–QB1
11. P–B3	N–Q5!!

Threatening mate and the Queen.

12. PxN	. . .

If 12. Q–Q1 R–B8! wins.

12. . . .	R–B7
13. N–B4	. . .

Or 13. Q–Q1 RxN and the threat of 14. . . . RxRP and 15. . . . R–R8 wins for Black.

13. . . .	Q–K3ch
14. N–K5	PxN
15. K–Q1	Q–B4!
Resigns	

A classic illustration of the attack on the uncastled King.

Attacks on the castled position, particularly on KR7, are indicated when the defender has not a Knight at KB3.

After 16. P–K5

Doroshkevich-Tal, U.S.S.R. 1975.

| 16. . . . | NPxP! |

The sacrifice of the piece is based on the availability of his remaining pieces for the attack and the shattered castled position of the White King.

17. PxN	RxB
18. PxB	N–K4
19. B–N2	Q–N4
20. N–K4	Q–R5
21. Q–Q2	KxP

In order to get the QR into the game.

| 22. Q–B2 | . . . |

Alarmed by the menace of 22. . . . R–R1, White loses back the piece. But an adequate defense seems lacking. If 22. QR–K1 R–R1 33. P–KR3 RxPch and Black forces mate.

| 22. . . . | QxQ |
| 23. RxQ | . . . |

If 23. NxQ P–B6 24. B–R3 R–K7 25. P–N3 R–R1 and Black has a winning position.

23. . . .	P–B6
24. NxQP	R–Q1
25. NxNP	PxBch
26. KxP	RxP
27. P–N3	N–Q6
28. R–B2	. . .

There is no safe square for the Rook. If 28. R–Q2 R–K8 wins the Exchange. And if 28. R/2–B1 R–N4ch 29. K–R1 R–K7 wins.

28. . . .	R–K8!!
Resigns	

Black wins a Rook. For example, 29. RxP (29. RxR NxRch wins) R/8xR! 30. RxR N–B5ch! 31. K–B3 NxR.

Demolish the enemy's castled position by a piece sacrifice!

After 19. . . . P–R3

Geller–Keres, U.S.S.R. 1973.

20. N–Q6! . . .

An active sacrifice.

| **20. . . .** | **PxB** |

Forced. If 20. . . . R–B1? 21. B/5xN QxB 22. NxB QRxN 23. QxN and White has a piece.

| **21. NxBP!** | **. . .** |

Demolition.

| **21. . . .** | **Q–R4** |

If 21. . . . KxN 22. NxNPch K–B3 (22. . . . K–N1 23. Q–N3ch wins the Queen) 23. N–R7ch K–B2 24. B–N3ch N–Q4 25. QxNch K–K2 26. Q–K6 mate. Or if 21. . . . Q–B2 22. N/7xNP N–KB3 23. B–N3ch with a winning attack for White.

| **22. N/7xNP** | **R–B1** |

If 22. . . . R–Q1 23. Q–N3ch K–R1 24. N–B7ch wins. So, Black returns the piece and hopes the attack abates.

| **23. BxN** | **QxRP** |
| **24. R–K2** | **Q–R6** |

With 24. . . . Q–Q4? 25. R–Q2! the Queen is trapped.

| **25. R–K3** | **Q–N5** |

The Queen goes again with 25. . . . Q–R7? 26. R–B2 Q–Q4 27. R–Q3.

| **25. BxB** | **QRxB** |
| **26. Q–Q7** | **. . .** |

Threatening 27. Q–K6ch K–R1 28. Q–R3ch K–N1 29. Q–R7 mate.

| **26. . . .** | **N–B4** |

Or 26. . . . KR–K1 27. Q–K6ch K–R1 28. N–B7ch K–R2 29. N/3–N5ch K–N1 30. N–R6ch K–R1 31. Q–N8ch RxQ 32. N/6–B7 mate.

| **27. Q–K6ch** | **K–R1** |
| **28. QxNP** | **Resigns** |

Know your pawn patterns! Consider their assets and liabilities when making your middlegame plans!

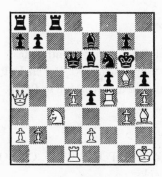

After 19. B–R3

Uhlmann–Larsen, Leningrad 1973.

19. . . .	**RxN!**

A maneuver, not a sacrifice, to obtain the superior Pawn structure.

20. PxR	**N–Q4**
21. BxB	**QxB**
22. R/1–KB1	**NxR**
23. RxN	**Q–QB2**

Applying pressure to the backward BP and NP.

24. P–Q5	**B–Q2**
25. Q–N4	**. . .**

Seeking 26. Q–K7 and 27. Q–N5ch.

25. . . .	**R–K1**
26. R–B1	**P–N3**
27. K–R2	**K–B3**

Preparing to use the KNP as a lever.

28. P–B4	P–N3
29. P–K3	R–QB1
30. R–B1	Q–K4!
31. B–B1	R–B4
32. Q–R3	P–KN4!
33. QxP??	. . .

A combination of Pawn hunger and a desire for some counter-play leads White fatally astray. 33. PxPch KxP 34. Q–B3 QxQ 35. RxQ P–N4! is also distinctly favorable to Black. But the alternatives are equally unpleasant.

| 33. . . . | Q–Q3! |

With 33. . . . PxP? 34. QxPch K–B2 35. QxR QxPch Black gets no more than a few checks.

| 34. R–N1 | P–N4 |
| 35. PxPch | . . . |

If 35. K–N2 PxP 36. PxP R–B1 and Black penetrates the KN-file.

35. . . .	KxP
36. K–N2	P–R5
37. PxPch	KxP
38. K–B2	PxP
39. Q–N8	. . .

And White lost on time. Otherwise Black would have won with 39. . . . QxQ 40. RxQ P–B6 41. R–N1 RxP.

Tactics is the most important element in the middlegame.

—Tarrasch

After 17. K–N2

Hug–Hort, Skopje 1972.

| 17. . . . | Q–R4! |

With the better position, one is morally obligated to attack!

| 18. P–KR3 | . . . |

Not 18. PxP? N–N5 19. B–N1 R–B7ch 20. BxR QxPch 21. K–B3 R–B1ch 22. KxN P–R4 mate!

18. . . .	Q–N3
19. QR–B1	R–B2
20. PxP	P–N5
21. P–KR4	P–K4!

To fix the doubled KPs. Black has a clear advantage.

| 22. Q–Q3 | . . . |

If 22. PxP PxP 23. K–R2 QR–KB1 24. N–Q3 NxP 25. NxP R–B7ch 26. BxR RxBch 27. K–N1 Q–B4 28. N–Q3 B–B4! wins.

22. . . .	NxP
23. N–B2	QR–KB1
23. B–N1	BxP!

To clear the sixth rank.

24. PxB   **R–B6!!**

All very imaginative—and precise!

24. N–K3   . . .

If 24. PxR PxPch 25. K–B1 Q–N7ch 26. K–K1 P–B7ch 27. K–K2
PxB=Q mate.

24. . . .   **R–N6ch**
25. K–R1   . . .

If 25. K–R2 Q–R4, justifying the Bishop sacrifice.

25. . . .   **R–B7!**
     Resigns

Black threatened 26. . . . R–R6ch 27. B–R2 R/7xBch with mate
to follow. If 26. BxR NxBch 27. K–R2 R–R6ch 28. K–N1 NxQ 29.
RxN Q–K5 wins easily.

A far-advanced passed pawn can throw the enemy game into disorder.

—Tarrasch

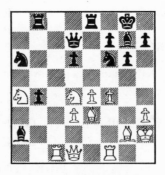

After 21. R–B1

Popov–Kavalek, Hoogoven 1976.

| 21. . . . | P–N6! |

The process of winning with a passed pawn is begun.

| 22. N–N2 | N–Q4! |

Now every last piece is directly or indirectly placed to assist in ramming through the QNP.

| 23. B–N1 | . . . |

After 23. PxN RxB White's pawns and dark squares are further weakened.

| 23. . . . | N/4–N5 |
| 24. Q–Q2 | N–B7! |

Wins another pawn.

| 25. P–K5 | . . . |

If 25. NxN? BxN! and Black wins a piece or the Exchange.

25. . . .	NxN
26. BxN	PxP
27. BxP	RxB!

The Exchange "sacrifice" serves to increase the pressure on the blockader and to gain additional control of the dark squares throughout the board.

28. PxR	BxPch
29. K–R1	Q–Q5
30. R–KB2	N–N5

Threatening 31. . . . QxN 32. QxQ BxQ 33. RxB NxP 34. R/1–QN1 BxR 35. RxB P–N7 and Black wins.

| 31. B–B1 | N–B7! |

Finally dislodging the blockader.

| 32. N–B4 | P–N7 |

33. NxP	B–Q4ch
34. B–N2	. . .

Or 34. K–N1 RxN 35. RxN RxR 36. QxR B–KN6 37. B–N2 BxB 38. KxB BxR 39. QxB QxP and the two-Pawn plus wins.

34. . . .	RxN
35. Q–R5	. . .

On 35. RxN RxR 36. QxR Q–R8ch 37. R–B1 QxR mates.

35. . . .	QxR
Resigns	

For if 36. QxB Q–N6 37. Q–Q8ch (37. K–N1 Q–R7ch 38. K–B2 N–N5ch wins) 37. . . . K–N2 and there is no defense to the threat of 38. . . . N–K6.

Every middlegame sacrifice and stratagem is not sound. And every refutation is not always found!

After 17. . . . N–K6

Szabo–Timman, Amsterdam 1976.

18. Q–R6!	. . .

Sound in the game, unsound in the post-mortem!

18. . . .	NxR
19. N–KN5	Q–K2
20. P–Q6!	. . .

Not 20. RxN? Q–N2!

20. . . .	Q–K6ch

Does White get compensation for the Exchange on 20. . . . Q–N2 21. B–B4ch K–R1 22. N–B7ch K–N1 23. RxN (23. N–N5ch draws) QxQ 24. NxQch K–R1 25. NxB PxN 26. RxP?

21. KxN	N–B1
22. R–Q1	R–K4?

There is a refutation in 22. . . . QR–Q1! 23. B–B4ch B–K3 24. N–Q5 Q–K4! 25. NxB RxN 26. N–B7 RxP 27. BxRch NxB 28. RxR QxR 29. NxN QxN and Black has a won Queen-and-Pawn Ending.

23. P–Q7	R–Q1
24. B–B4ch	B–K3
25. NxB!	R–B4ch?

Best is 25. . . . QxQ 26. NxRch K–N2 27. N–K6ch RxN 28. P–Q8=Q Q–B5ch 29. K–N1 QxB 30. Q–B7ch K–R1 31. QxNP Q–QN5 although White would have the better Pawn formation.

But not 25. . . . NxN? 26. QxQ RxQ 27. N–Q5 R–K4 28. N–B7 K–B2 29. NxN RxN 30. R–K1 and White emerges a piece up.

26. N–B4ch	K–R1
27. N/3–Q5	Q–K5
28. B–K2	N–K3?

Black misses his last chance to save the game, 28. . . . P–KN4!

29. B–B3	Q–B5ch
30. K–N1	NxN
31. N–K3	Q–K3
32. NxR	QxN
33. R–K1!	N–K3

Otherwise 34. R–K8ch wins.

34. B–N4   **Resigns**

Seventeen pressure moves finally win a piece.

In a mating attack material is of secondary importance.

—Fine

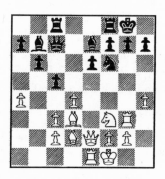

After 15. . . . N–B3

Hoshino–Torre, Manila 1975.

16. N–N5!   . . .

Now all the White pieces are poised for a direct attack on the Dark Monarch.

16. . . .   **P–N3**

If 16. . . . P–B5 17. BxPch NxB 18. NxN KxN 19. Q–R5ch K–N1 20. RxPch KxR 21. B–R6ch K–R2 22. B–B4ch K–N1 23. BxQ RxB 24. Q–K5 KR–B1 25. R–K3 and White has a decisive mating attack.

17. NxKP!   . . .

Black defended against a sacrifice at his KR2 but was unable to ward off similar ones at K3 and KN3!

17. . . .	PxN
18. QxPch	R–B2
19. BxP!	PxB
20. RxPch	K–B1
21. B–R6ch	K–K1
22. RxN	. . .

The sacrifices begin to pay off.

22. . . .	B–Q4
23. Q–B5	. . .

Not 23. QxB?? RxR and Black is a Rook up.

23. . . .	RxR
24. QxR	. . .

Threatening to win the KB with 25. B–N5.

24. . . .	K–Q1
25. Q–N7	. . .

Threatening to win the Queen with 26. RxB QxR 27. B–N5.

25. . . .	B–B5ch
26. K–N1	BxP
27. B–N5ch!	BxB
28. QxBch	K–Q2
29. R–K7ch	. . .

Justifying the 17th and 19th moves.

29. . . .	K–B3
30. RxQch, and White won.	

An attack on the King is not merely fascinating in itself, but it is also highly profitable.

—Kotov

After 12. . . . P–K4

Collins–Ed. Lasker, New York 1960.

| 13. PxP | . . . |

The refutation of Black's premature Pawn break begins.

13. . . .	NxP
14. NxN	BxN
15. Q–R5	. . .

The scantly covered King and the loose piece are ready targets.

| 15. . . . | B–B4 |

An ingenious way of saving the KB. If 15. . . . B–B2? 16. QxBPch RxQ 17. R–K8 mate. And if 15. . . . Q–B4 16. B–Q3 wins.

| 16. P–N4! | . . . |

Not 16. QxB?? BxPch 17. KxB QxQ and Black wins.

| 16. . . . | P–KN3 |

The only way to save a Bishop.

| 17. Q–N5 | P–KR3 |

Again the only way.

| 18. QxP | B–N2? |

If 18. ... BxNP? 19. QxPch K–R1 20. Q–R6ch K–N1 21. Q–N5ch K–R2 22. RxB wins. If 18. ... BxBP? 19. BxB QxB 20. QR–B1 Q–N2 21. QxQch KxQ 22. PxB wins. Best is 18. ... B–B7.

19. Q–N5	Q–B2
20. B–N3	B–Q6
21. R–K3	. . .

Again with the King and loose piece in mind.

21. . . .	QR–Q1
22. R–R3	KR–K1
23. Q–R4	R–K7

Black has managed to complete his development and assume an aggressive attitude, but it is the vulnerability of his King that proves fatal.

| 24. Q–R7ch | K–B1 |
| 25. B–R6 | . . . |

Threatening 26. Q–R8ch.

25. . . .	BxB
26. QxBch	K–K1
27. Q–N5!	. . .

Threatening to win the Bishop.

| 27. . . . | Q–K2 |

There is no saving move.

28. R–R8ch	K–Q2
29. RxRch	KxR
30. Q–Q5ch	Resigns

For if 30. ... Q–Q2 31. QxQch KxQ 32. R–Q1 wins the Bishop.

The Opening

Develop all your pieces!
Develop them rapidly!
Develop them to get control of the center!
Develop with a plan!
Develop to seize the initiative!

These five imperatives, expressed in various ways, summarize the accumulated wisdom of opening theory over the last hundred years, and they govern the play of every master, be he classicist, hypermodern, eclectic, or modern.

Then follow more practical, specific rules:

Open with 1. P–K4 or 1. P–Q4.
Make only a few Pawn moves.
Avoid useless, weakening Pawn moves.
Develop Knights before Bishops, usually at KB3 and QB3.
Wait to see which is the best diagonal for the Bishop.
Find open files for the Rooks.
Do not make early Queen sorties.
Castle early, usually on the Kingside, to safeguard the King.
Do not sacrifice material recklessly.
Do not rely on traps.
Always assume your opponent will make the correct reply.

Advice such as this—remembering always that chess is a game of exceptions—is ignored by the average player at his peril.

Some knowledge of all the openings broadens one's outlook. Specializing in a few is practical. Varying now and then is stimulating. In study, opined Mason, the Opening comes last, after the Middlegame and Ending. Colors? **"When I have the White pieces, I win because I am White; when I have the Black pieces, I win because I am Bogolyubov,"** said that great great Russian-Polish grandmaster. Memorizing book variations? A horror. Understanding them is the ideal. Lasker touched on it years ago when he wrote: **"Show me three variations in the leading handbook on the Openings and I will show you two of those three that are defective."**

Fischer's fifth move, regarded as inferior, and his sixth (the customary follow-up) prepared no one for the gambit which he introduced on move seven.

—Evans

Fischer–Gligoric, Havana 1966.

Ruy Lopez

1.	P–K4	P–K4
2.	N–KB3	N–QB3
3.	B–N5	P–QR3

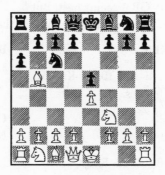

4. BxN!   . . .

The Exchange Variation. The text, 5. O–O, and 7. P–B3 constitute the Fischer Variation, a revival and refinement of the Lasker and Barendregt variations.

4. . . .	**QPxB**

It has long been known that 4. . . . NPxB 5. P–Q4 PxP 6. QxP favors White.

5. O–O!	**. . .**

Posing the problem of how to protect the Black KP. 5. P–Q4 PxP 6. QxP QxQ 7. NxQ B–Q2 has received most attention.

5. . . .	**P–B3**

Feasible alternatives are 5. . . . Q–Q3! 6. P–Q4 PxP 7. NxP N–K2 and 5. . . . B–KN5 6. P–KR3 P–KR4!?

6. P–Q4	**B–KN5!**

Not 6. . . . PxP? 7. NxP B–Q3 8. Q–R5ch P–N3 8. Q–B3 BxPch 9. KxB QxN 10. R–Q1! and White has all the play for a doubled Pawn.

7. P–B3!	**. . .**

Gligoric's own suggested gambit!

7. . . .	**PxP**
8. PxP	**Q–Q2**

Gligoric's 8. . . . P–QB4! seems best. But 8. . . . BxN? 9. QxB QxP 10. R–Q1 Q–B5 11. B–B4 again gives White the play.

9. P–KR3!	**B–K3?**

Correct is 9. . . . B–R4! 10. N–K5! BxQ 11. NxQ KxN 12. RxB R–K1 with equal chances.

10. N–B3	**O–O–O**
11. B–B4!	**N–K2?**

Better is 11. . . . B–Q3 12. BxB QxB.

12. R–B1	**N–N3**

| 13. B–N3 | B–Q3 |
| 14. N–QR4! | BxB? |

Black should avoid weakening QB4 and play 14. . . . K–N1.

| 15. PxB | K–N1 |

If 15. . . . P–N3? 16. P–Q5! PxP 17. NxPch wins.

| 16. N–B5 | Q–Q3 |
| 17. Q–R4! | . . . |

Threatening, among several other things, 18. Q–N4.

| 17. . . . | K–R2?? |

The defense 17. . . . B–B1! 18. R–B3 N–B1! offers hope.

| 18. NxRP! | . . . |

Decisive. Black bowed out on the 25th move. If 18. . . . PxN 19. RxP and White mates or wins the Queen.

In the "Technical System" Black gives his opponent the center while answering the question of where to place his Queen Bishop.

—Taimanov

Karpov–Portisch, Portoroz Slav Defense 1975.

1. N–KB3	P–Q4
2. P–Q4	N–KB3
3. P–B4	P–B3
4. N–B3	PxP
5. P–QR4	B–B4

This is the Dutch Variation, or Technical System.

| 6. P–K3 | P–K3 |

| 7. BxP | B–QN5 |
| 8. O–O | O–O |

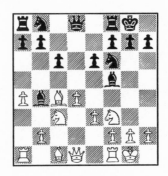

| 9. N–R4 | . . . |

Rarely tried, this variation wins the minor Exchange and provides play on the light squares.

| 9. . . . | B–N5 |

Trying to preserve the QB. If 9. . . . QN–Q2 10. P–B3 B–N3 11. P–K4 P–K4 12. PxP QNxP 13. B–K2 secures White the advantage.

| 10. P–B3 | B–R4 |

On 10. . . . N–Q4? 11. PxB! QxN 12. Q–B3! Q–Q1! 13. B–Q2 B–K2 14. B–K1 N–R3 15. B–B2 N/3–N5 16. P–K4 N–N3 17. B–QN3 R–B1 18. QR–Q1 White has the better center, better development, and the two Bishops.

11. P–N4	B–N3
12. NxB	RPxN
13. Q–N3!?	Q–K2

Likewise, 13. . . . Q–N3 14. R–Q1 R–Q1 15. P–N5 N–Q4 16. P–K4 favors White.

| 14. P–N5 | N–Q4 |

On 14. . . . KN–Q2 White prevents . . . P–K4 with 15. P–B4!

| 15. P–K4 | N–N3 |
| 16. N–R2! | B–R4 |

If 16. . . . NxB 17. NxB!

17. B–K2	P–K4
18. Q–B2!	N/3–Q2

White wins the Exchange with 18. . . . PxP? 19. P–N4! BxP 20. NxB QxN 21. B–R3.

19. PxP	QxP
20. K–R1	R–K1
21. B–QB4!	. . .

And with control of the center and superior development, White is in control and won on his 32nd move. After 21. B–QB4 the two main threats are 22. Q–N3 and 22. P–N4! QxR? 23. B–N2.

If the defender is forced to give up the center, then every possible attack follows almost of itself.
—Tarrasch

Spassky–Tal, Tallinn 1973.

Nimzo-Indian Defense

1. P–Q4	N–KB3
2. P–QB4	P–K3
3. N–QB3	B–N5
4. B–N5	. . .

A Spassky favorite.

4. . . .	P–KR3
5. B–R4	P–B4!
6. P–Q5	P–QN4!

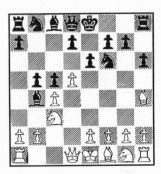

Tal shock treatment. "Book" is 6. . . . P–Q3.

| **7. QPxP?** | . . . |

Voluntarily giving up the center to gain a pawn. 7. P–K4 is natural.

| 7. . . . | **BPxP** |
| **8. PxP** | **P–Q4!** |

Establishing a massive, mobile pawn center and varying from the book 8. . . . Q–R4.

| **9. P–K3** | **O–O** |
| **10. N–B3?** | . . . |

Better are 10. P–QR3 and 10. B–Q3.

| 10. . . . | **Q–R4** |
| **11. BxN** | **RxB** |

Black's superior development and menacing pawn center more than compensate for the Pawn minus.

| **12. Q–Q2** | . . . |

More precise is 12. Q–B1 in order to be able to answer 12. . . . RxN 13. PxR P–Q5 14. PxP PxP with 15. P–QR3. After the text, Black develops the threat of . . . RxN combined with . . . P–Q5.

12. . . .	**P–R3!**
13. PxP	**N–B3!**
14. B–K2	**P–Q5!**

15. PxP	RxN!
16. BxR	PxP
17. O–O	. . .

If 17. BxN? PxN wins.

17. . . .	PxN
18. PxP	BxBP
19. Q–Q6	RxP
20. BxN	B–N5!
21. Q–N8	RxB

And with better attacking chances, Black won after seventeen more exciting moves.

To study opening variations without reference to the strategic concepts that develop from them in the middlegame, is, in effect, to separate the head from the body.

—Petrosian

Petrosian–Balashov, U.S.S.R. 1974.

Nimzo-Indian Defense

1. P–QB4	N–KB3
2. N–QB3	P–K3
3. P–Q4	B–N5
4. P–K3	P–B4
5. B–Q3	P–Q4
6. N–B3	O–O
7. O–O	QPxP

Better is 7. . . . N–B3 8. P–QR3 QPxP.

8. BxP	N–B3
9. B–Q3!	. . .

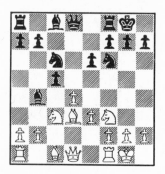

A novelty, 9. P–QR3 being usual.

	9. . . .	PxP
10. PxP		B–K2

Of course not 10. . . . NxP?? 11. NxN QxN 12. BxPch KxB 13. QxQ and White has a Queen for a Bishop.

11. R–K1	P–QN3

If 11. . . . N–QN5 12. B–N1 P–QN3 13. P–QR3 N/5–Q4 14. Q–Q3 B–N2 15. B–N5! threatening to win a piece with 16. NxN and 17. BxN.

12. P–QR3	B–N2
13. B–B2	R–B1
14. Q–Q3	R–K1?

Better is 14. . . . P–N3 15. B–R6 R–K1 16. QR–Q1 B–B1 17. BxB RxB, although White continues vigorously with 18. N–KN5 and 19. Q–R3.

15. P–Q5!	PxP

If 15. . . . N–QR4 16. PxP QxQ 17. PxPch KxP 18. N–K5ch K–N1 19. BxQ and White has a Pawn plus.

16. B–N5	N–K5

If 16. . . . P–N3? 17. RxB! QxR 18. NxP wins.

17. NxN	PxN
18. QxP	P–N3

19. Q–KR4	Q–B2
20. B–N3!	P–KR4
21. Q–K4	K–N2
22. BxP!	KxB
23. B–R6!	. . .

And Black resigned five moves later.

Never move a piece twice before you have moved every piece once.

—Anonymous

Ljubojevic–Durao, Orense 1974.

Ruy Lopez

1. P–K4	P–K4
2. N–KB3	N–QB3
3. B–N5	B–B4

The Classical Defense, long out of favor.

| 4. O–O | N–Q5? |

Never move a piece . . .

5. NxN	BxN
6. P–B3	B–N3
7. P–Q4	P–QB3
8. B–R4	P–Q3
9. N–R3!	B–B2

If 9. . . . N–B3 10. B–KN5 P–KR3 11. BxN QxB 12. P–Q5 B–Q2 13. N–B4 B–B2 14. PxP PxP 15. Q–Q3 and White has telling pressure on the backward QP.

| 10. P–Q5! | . . . |

An improvement on the customary 10. B–B2 and 10. P–KB4.

    10. . . .   **B–Q2**

If 10. . . . P–QN4 11. B–N3 B–N2 12. PxP BxP 13. B–Q5! BxB 14. QxB P–QR3 15. B–N5 gives White a clear plus.

    11. PxP   **PxP**

On 11. . . . BxP, White switches to the Kingside with 12. BxBch PxB 13. Q–N4 Q–B3 14. P–KB4.

12. N–B4	**Q–K2**
13. P–B4!	**N–B3**
14. PxP	**PxP**
15. P–QN3!	**B–N3ch**
16. K–R1	**NxP**
17. B–R3	**Q–K3**

Threatening 18. . . . N–N6ch 19. PxN Q–R3ch 20. Q–R5 QxQ mate.

    18. Q–Q3!   **P–KB4**

On 18. . . . N–B7ch 19. RxN BxR 20. N–Q6ch K–Q1 21. Q–B3 wins.

19. QR–K1!	**B–B2**
20. RxP!	**QxR**
21. RxN	. . .

And with attacking chances all over the board, White won after

21. ... O–O–O 22. N–Q6ch BxN 23. Q–R6ch! K–B2 24. QxRPch
K–B1 25. B–N5!

**I scored a success with my original 12. QN–Q2,
but of course it's too early to know whether this
move is more than a flash in the pan.**

—R. Byrne

R. Byrne–Matanovic, Biel 1976.

Ruy Lopez

1.	P–K4	P–K4
2.	N–KB3	N–QB3
3.	B–N5	P–QR3
4.	B–R4	N–B3
5.	O–O	B–K2
6.	R–K1	P–QN4
7.	B–N3	P–Q3
8.	P–B3	O–O
9.	P–KR3	N–N1

This is the flexible Breyer Variation. The older Tchigorin Variation continues 9. ... N–QR4 10. B–B2 P–B4.

10.	P–Q4	QN–Q2
11.	P–B4	P–B3
12.	QN–Q2!	. . .

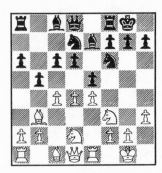

A new idea. White protects the QBP again in order to play 13. B–B2 and 14. P–QN4. 12. N–B3 is normal.

12. . . .	B–N2
13. B–B2	N–K1!
14. Q–K2!	. . .

A chess player has a right to change his (her) mind. If White bulls ahead with 14. P–QN4? then 14. . . . KPxP! 15. NxP B–B3 16. N/2–B3, and Black wins the Exchange with 16. . . . P–B4 17. NPxP QPxP.

14. . . .	Q–N3
15. N–N3	P–QB4
16. P–Q5	. . .

Achieving a spatial advantage.

| 16. . . . | P–N3 |
| 17. B–Q2 | . . . |

Threatening to win a precious little one with 18. B–R5 Q–R2 19. PxP PxP 20. QxP.

17. . . .	P–N5
18. B–R6	N–N2
19. QN–Q2	N–B3
20. P–N4!	K–R1
21. N–B1	N–N1
22. B–Q2	B–B1
23. N–N3	B–Q2

24. K–R2	P–QR4
25. R–KN1	. . .

By converting his spatial advantage and Kingside attacking chances, White won the Ending in sixty moves.

Opening theory develops further with each tournament. New variations are constantly being discovered and given practical trials. Analytic skill increases.

—Keres

Lombardy–Quinteros, Manila 1973.

Sicilian Defense

1. P–K4	P–QB4
2. N–KB3	P–Q3
3. P–Q4	PxP
4. NxP	N–KB3
5. N–QB3	P–QR3

The Najdorf Variation—which Lombardy likes to play and play against.

6. B–N5	P–K3
7. P–B4	B–K2
8. Q–B3	P–R3

Or 8. . . . Q–B2 immediately.

9. B–R4	Q–B2
10. O–O–O	QN–Q2
11. B–K2!	. . .

Not merely a developing move, it rushes the KB and KR into the attack.

11. . . .	R–QN1

If 11. . . . P–QN4?! 12. P–K5!

| 12. Q–N3 | R–N1?! |

Or perhaps 12. . . . P–QN4!?

| 13. KR–B1! | P–QN4? |

A new try which meets an instant, violent refutation.

| 14. NxKP!! | . . . |

New variations are constantly being discovered. . . .

| 14. . . . | PxN |
| 15. Q–N6ch | K–Q1 |

Or 15. . . . K–B1 16. P–K5! PxP 17. P–B5 P–K5 18. BxN PxB
(18. . . . NxB 19. B–R5! NxB 20. PxPch B–B3 21. R–Q8ch wins) 19.
Q–RPch R–N2 20. PxP and White wins.

| 16. P–K5 | PxP |

Or 16. . . . N–K1 17. QxKP wins.

| 17. P–B5! | PxP |

If 17. . . . Q–B3 18. BxN BxB 19. B–B3 Q–N3 20. PxP QxP 21.
B–Q5! B–N4ch 22. QxBch PxQ 23. BxQ R–K1 24. B–N4 and White
has a winning position.

| 18. BxN | BxB |
| 19. N–Q5 | Q–B3 |

| 20. RxP | R–B1 |
| 21. B–N4! | . . . |

And the concluding moves were 21. . . . R–N3 22. RxB! PxR 23. Q–N7 R–N2 24. Q–K7 mate. A brilliancy-prize game, for one thousand dollars.

The art of treating the opening stage of the game correctly and without error is basically the art of using time efficiently.

—Gligoric

Hübner–G. Padron, Las Palmas 1976.

Benoni Defense

| 1. N–KB3 | P–QB4 |
| 2. P–B4 | . . . |

Declining the invitation to make it a Sicilian with 2. P–K4.

2. . . .	N–KB3
3. N–B3	P–KN3
4. P–Q4	B–N2
5. P–Q5	. . .

Reaching the Benoni by transposition. If 5. PxP? Q–R4!

5. . . .	P–Q3
6. P–K4	O–O
7. B–K2	P–K3

Standard strategy: open the K-file and obtain a Queenside Pawn majority.

| 8. O–O | PxP |
| 9. BPxP | . . . |

More dynamic than 9. KPxP.

9.	. . .	R–K1
10.	N–Q2	QN–Q2
11.	R–K1!	. . .

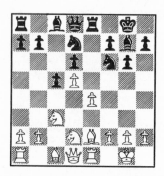

Usual is 11. P–B3, making the KP rock safe. But White proposes to advance his BP to B4 in one move not two!

11.	. . .	P–QR3
12.	P–QR4	Q–B2
13.	P–R3!	. . .

Informing Black that his position is bankrupt!

13.	. . .	P–KN4?

Desperate and suicidal. But if 13. . . . N–K4 14. P–B4! forces the ignominious 14. . . . N/4–Q2.

14.	N–B4	P–R3

If 14. . . . NxKP 15. NxN RxN 16. BxP and Black's Kingside is fractured.

15.	P–B4!	. . .

A tempo saved is a tempo earned!

15.	. . .	NxKP?

Relatively best is 15. . . . N–R2.

16.	B–Q3	B–Q5ch

If 16. . . . N/5–B3 17. RxRch NxR 18. PxP PxP 19. BxP wins.

17. K–R2	BxN
18. PxB	N/2–B3
19. PxP	PxP
20. Q–B3!	. . .

And the conclusion to this anti-Benoni system was 20. . . . P–N5 (20. . . . Q–K2 21. BxP NxB 22. Q–N3 wins) 21. Q–B4 NxQP 22. RxN! NxQ 23. RxRch K–N2 24. BxN Q–Q2 25. NxP PxP 26. R–KN1 QxP 27. PxPch, Black resigns.

Your only task in the opening is to reach a playable middlegame.
—Portisch

Portisch–Donner, Wijk aan Zee 1975.

King's Indian Defense

1. P–QB4	N–KB3
2. N–QB3	P–KN3
3. P–Q4	B–N2
4. P–K4	O–O
5. B–K3	. . .

5. P–K5? boomerangs with 5. . . . N–K1, 6. . . . P–Q3, and 7. . . . P–QB4, undermining White's center.

| 5. . . . | P–Q3 |
| 6. P–B3 | . . . |

The old reliable Sämisch Variation.

| 6. . . . | P–K4 |
| 7. P–Q5 | P–B3 |

Designed to discourage White from castling long and launching a Kingside pawn roller (P–KN4).

8.	B–Q3	PxP
9.	BPxP	N–K1
10.	Q–Q2	P–B4
11.	PxP!	. . .

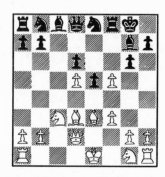

Polugaevsky's program (along with 8. B–Q3), which unfreezes the center, weakens Black's flank position, and prevents 11. . . . P–B5! and a Black Kingside expansion.

11.	. . .	PxP
12.	KN–K2	N–Q2
13.	O–O	N–B4
14.	B–QB2	P–QR4
15.	P–B4!	. . .

This forces open either the KB-file or the QR1–KR8 diagonal.

15.	. . .	PxP?

Better is 15. . . . P–K5. Then, however, White can prepare to break with P–QN4 or P–KN4.

16.	NxP	B–K4
17.	QR–K1	Q–B3
18.	N–R3	P–N3
19.	B–N5	Q–N3
20.	B–B4	B–B3
21.	R–B3!	. . .

With the advantage in time and space and a direct attack against the King, White took the decision in the middlegame with 21. . . .

K–R1 22. R–N3 Q–R4 23. B–Q1 Q–R5 24. N–KN5 N–K5 25. N/5xN PxN 26. NxP, Black resigns. If 26. . . . QxB 27. QxQ B–Q5ch 28. N–B2! RxQ 29. RxNch R–B1 30. RxR mate.

> **As opening theory develops, the role of the initiative is being more and more closely analyzed.**
> **—Suetin**

Diesen–Rohde, Memphis 1976.

Pirc Defense

1. P–K4	P–Q3
2. P–Q4	P–KN3
3. N–KB3	N–KB3
4. N–B3	B–N2
5. B–K2	O–O
6. O–O	P–B3
7. P–KR3	. . .

Preventing 7. . . . B–N5 and providing a possible haven for the QB.

7. . . .	P–QN4
8. P–K5	. . .

The role of the initiative . . .

8. . . .	N–K1
9. B–KB4	B–N2
10. Q–Q2!	. . .

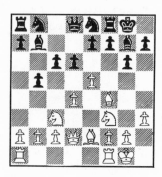

An improvement on the book 10. R–K1. White takes advantage of the fact that Black has no practical way of preserving his defensive, fianchettoed KB.

10. . . .	N–Q2
11. KR–Q1	N–N3
12. B–R6	Q–B2
13. BxB	NxB?

After 13. . . . KxB White cannot get to KR6 with his Queen, but the dark squares in the fianchettoed position remain weak.

| 14. B–Q3 | P–B3 |
| 15. Q–R6! | Q–Q2 |

Of course if 15. . . . QPxP 16. PxP PxP?? 17. N–N5 and White mates in two.

| 16. R–K1 | R–B2 |

If 16. . . . N–B4? 17. BxN QxB? 18. PxQP PxP 19. R–K7 R–B2 20. RxR KxR 21. QxRPch wins.

| 17. N–KR4 | N–K3 |
| 18. R–K3! | QPxP |

The plausible 18. . . . NxP?? loses to 19. NxKNP! PxN 20. BxKNP R–N2 21. P–K6! NxKP 22. B–B5.

19. PxP	P–KB4
20. R–Q1	N–Q4
21. R–N3!	QR–KB1?

Loses. The only chance is to bolster the castled setup with 21. . . . N–B1 or 21. . . . N–N2.

22. BxBP! . . .

And the continuation was 22. . . . RxB 23. NxKNP! K–B2! 24. QxPch K–K1 25. NxN PxN 26. NxR NxN 27. Q–R6 RxKP 28. R–KB3 R–B4 29. R/1–Q3 P–Q5 30. RxP QxR 31. RxR N–Q2 32. RxP B–K5 33. P–B3, and Black resigned on move 49.

Tactical Play

"Chess is 99 per cent tactics," wrote Teichmann, and Tarrasch said, "Tactics is the most important element in the middle-game." And Evans, in a glossary of terms, defines "tactics" as: "Immediate schemes, traps and threats deemed necessary for executing a strategical plan. Combinations are tactical, though their objectives may be strategical or positional." Tactical methods—pinning, forking, double attacks, skewering, and checking—are devices to bring about checkmate or the winning of material. They decide most games, at every level of skill.

Is there a difference between tactical play and combinations? Seemingly there is not, but actually there is, although the similarity is obvious and the difference may be in degree rather than in kind. A combination is apt to be more inspiring, deeper, dramatic, decisive, and always involves one or more sacrifices. Tactical play provides more immediate results, forces transitions, clarifies positions, employs traps, has a give-and-take quality, and is free of sacrifices, except those of a momentary nature. But both combinations and tactical play are based on the lively activity of the pieces.

Tal is the great modern exponent of tactical play, the successor to Morphy and Alekhine, the patron saint of all players who prefer exciting, speculative chess. He is a killer and uses the pieces as weapons. Like Marshall, he is primarily tactical and a crowd pleaser and frankly admits, "I love to hear the spectators react!"

Tal is always on the look-out for some spectacular sacrifice. He is not so much interested in who has the better game, or in the essential soundness of his own game, but in finding that one shot, that dramatic breakthrough that will give him the win.
—Fischer

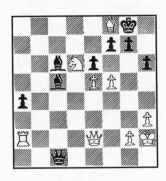

After 42. BxR

Botterill–Tal, Bath 1973.

| 42. . . . | **B–K6!!** |

Down material Tal naturally plays for mate. Threat: 43. . . . B–B5ch 44. P–N3 Q–B8 mate.

| **43. K–N3** | . . . |

If 43. P–R4 B–B5ch 44. K–R3 Q–B6ch 45. K–N4 Q–N6ch 46. K–R5 P–N3ch 47. PxP PxP mate.

| 43. . . . | **B–KN4** |

Threatening 44. . . . Q–B5 mate.

| **44. Q–B4** | . . . |

If 44. Q–N4? P–R4! mates or wins the Queen.

| 44. . . . | **Q–K6ch** |
| **45. K–N4** | . . . |

Forced, for if 45. K–R2 B–B5ch 46. K–R1 Q–K8ch 47. Q–B1 QxQ mate.

45. . . .	**B–R5!!**
46. B–K7!	. . .

Again forced, for if 46. KxB Q–N4 mate.

46. . . .	**BxB**
47. NxP	. . .

If 47. QxB P–R4ch 48. KxP Q–N4 mate.

47. . . .	**P–R4ch**
48. KxP	**B–K1!**

Once more threatening mate at KN4.

49. K–N4	**PxPch**
50. KxP	**P–N3ch**
51. K–N4	. . .

If 50. KxP Q–N4 mate, and if 50. K–K6 BxNch wins the Queen.

51. . . .	**B–Q2ch**
Resigns	

The Queen and Rook were about to disappear.

In chess—as in any conflict—success lies in attack.

—Euwe

After 26. N–N5

Halprin–Pillsbury, Vienna 1898.

| 26. . . . | P–B5! |
| 27. Q–R3 | . . . |

If 27. PxP Q–N3 28. K–B1 B–R6ch 29. RxB Q–N8 mate.

| 27. . . . | P–K6 |

Threatening 28. . . . KPxP 29. BxN R–K6! 30. BxB QxB 31. Q–N4 QxPch 32. K–B1 P–B6 and mate in two.

| 28. P–Q6 | N–K4 |

Or 28. . . . KPxP. The text threatens both 29. . . . BxB and 29. . . . P–B6ch.

| 29. BxN | . . . |

If 29. BxB P–B6ch 30. K–N1 PxPch 31. KxP NxBch wins.

| 29. . . . | P–B6ch! |

An important zwischenzug.

| 30. K–R2 | RxB |
| 31. B–Q3 | B–Q2! |

Vacating KN5 for the Queen.

32. PxP	Q–N5
33. B–B1	. . .

Necessary to prevent mate.

33. . . .	R–R4!

Threatening 34. . . . RxPch! 35. PxR QxPch 36. K–N1 Q–N6ch 37. B–N2 QxB mate.

34. R–B2	. . .

Nothing helps. On 34. Q–N2 BxN 35. PxB RxPch 36. PxR BxPch 37. Q–K5 BxQ mate follows.

34. . . .	RxN
35. R–Q2	R–K4
36. Q–N2	RxKP
Resigns	

Else Black, a Bishop to the good, might end it with 37. QxP B–B3 38. Q–N2 P–B7 39. RxP QxNP mate.

Attack! Always attack!

—Anderssen

After 16. R–K3

Quinteros–Portisch, Manila 1974.

Black is about to gain the Exchange. But winning the game still requires tactical, attacking play.

16. . . .		R–K1
17. N–Q5		B–QB4

The Exchange will not run away.

18. P–QN4!		PxP e.p.
19. B–R3!		BxRch

Not 19. . . . BxB?? 20. RxRch QxR 21. N–B6ch and Black loses his Queen.

20. NxB		P–N7!
21. R–N1		. . .

If 21. QxQ? PxR=Q 22. Q–Q2 R–N8 and the double Exchange advantage soon wins.

21. . . .		Q–N4
22. Q–K2		Q–QR4!

Every move an attacking move!

23. BxP		QxP

Threatening 24. . . . B–B4.

24. Q–B2		RxN!
25. KxR		B–B4
26. B–K4		Q–N6ch!

Decisive simplification. But 26. . . . R–K1?? allows White to get back in business with 27. Q–B3! RxBch 28. K–B3!

27. QxQ		RxQch
28. K–B4		BxB

The Bishops-of-opposite-colors ending (28. . . . R–N5 29. B–B6! RxBch 30. K–B3 R–K6ch! 31. KxR BxR) is also a win for Black.

29. KxB		P–QR4

And the continuation was 30. P–R4 P–R4 31. K–B4 P–R5 32. R–QB1 RxB 33. RxP P–R6 34. R–R7 P–R7 35. P–N4 R–N5ch 36. K–N5 RxPch 37. K–R6 K–B1 38. RxP RxP and White resigned.

Expeditious return of material is a mark of the master.

—Eckstrom

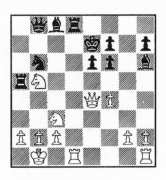

After 18. N/6–N5

Balashov–Polugaevsky, Manila 1976.

18. . . .	RxN!

An Exchange to turn the tide.

19. NxR	N–Q4
20. P–B4	B–R3
21. PxN	QxN!

At the cost of the Exchange, Black has transformed a defensive position into an attacking one.

22. KR–K1	B–QN2
23. QxP	BxQP!
24. QxB	R–QN1
25. R–Q2	. . .

Now the Queen's absence is felt. If 25. P–QN3?? BxQNP 26. PxB QxPch 27. K–B1 Q–N7 mate.

25. . . .	BxPch!
26. K–B1	. . .

If 26. KxB Q–R4ch 27. K–N1 QxR and Black forces mate.

26. . . .	R–B1ch
27. R–B2	RxRch
28. KxR	Q–B5ch
29. K–Q2	Q–N5ch
30. K–K2	B–B5ch
31. K–Q1	. . .

On 31. K–B2 Q–Q7ch wins the Rook.

31. . . .	QxP
32. R–K5	. . .

Black threatened 32. . . . B–N6 mate. If 32. R–K3 Q–Q5ch and if 32. R–K4 Q–N8ch winning the Rook in both cases.

32. . . .	PxR
33. Q–N5ch	K–Q2
Resigns	

A piece is too much.

**Never is cold reason, clear thinking, more neces-
sary than when victory is in sight.**

—**Znosko-Borovsky**

After 27. BxBP

Liberzon–Larsen, Biel 1976.

27. . . .		**B–QB3!**

Black begins to work out of a cramped position with a few deft
tactical shots.

28. P–N6		. . .

Of course not 28. PxB?? QxRch and Black wins.

28. . . .		**R–Q1**

Threatening to win the Exchange with 29. . . . B–K5.

29. R–B3		**B–K5**
30. R–N2		. . .

If 30. B–Q3?? RxB! 31. RxR P–B5 wins.

30. . . .		**Q–B3**
31. B–N5		**Q–R1**
32. B–Q3		**P–R6!**

An unpleasant surprise!

33. R–N1?		. . .

If 33. BxB? PxR 34. BxQ P–N8=Qch 35. R–B1 QxRP wins. Relatively best is 33. R–N5 BxB 34. RxB Q–B3 35. RxRch BxR, although Black will win the QNP and be an extra QBP ahead.

33. . . .	RxB!
34. RxR	P–B5
35. R–Q7	. . .

There are no longer any answers. If 35. P–N7 BxP 36. R–KN3 BxPch 37. RxB RxRch wins.

35. . . .	BxR
36. RxB	RxP
37. QxP	BxP!
Resigns	

After 38. QxB R–N7 39. Q–R1 RxB 40. Q–KN1 P–R7 41. R–R7 QxR! 42. QxQ R–Q8ch 43. Q–N1 P–R8=Q Black mates in three.

If I win, it was a sacrifice. If I lose, then it was a mistake.

—Koltanowski

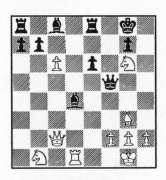

After 18. . . . Q–KB4

Velimirovic–Kholmov, Yugoslavia–U.S.S.R. 1975.

19. Q–N3 . . .

Not 19. QxQ PxQ 20. RxB?? R–K8 mate.

19. . . .	QxN
20. RxB	PxP
21. P–R3	Q–B4
22. N–Q2	P–B4
23. R–KN4	. . .

Having sacrificed a Pawn earlier, White intends to prove it was not a mistake by mounting an attack on KN7.

23. . . .	R–K2
24. B–Q6	R–KB2
25. Q–N3	B–N2
26. B–K5	Q–R2

The only balm for the sore spot.

27. N–B4	B–Q4
28. N–Q6	R–Q2
29. P–B4	P–B5
30. K–R2	R–N1
31. P–B5!	R–N6

If 31. . . . PxP? 32. R–R4! P–B5! 33. Q–N4! wins. Tactics!

32. Q–B4!	. . .

Menacing 33. P–B6 and wins.

32. . . .	BxP

A desperate trick.

33. P–R4!	. . .

If 33. KxB (or 33. RxB) QxPch and Black has some counterplay.

33. . . .	B–R6

Or 33. . . . B–Q4 34. N–K8! and White wins.

34. QxP!	BxR

Or 34. . . . R–N1 35. QxPch K–R1 36. RxP! RxR 37. N–B7ch
K–N1 38. N–N5ch K–R1 39. NxQ wins.

35. Q–B8ch   **Resigns**

Mate next move.

**The old aphorism holds good, that after an attack
has been repulsed, the counterattack is generally
decisive.**

—Reti

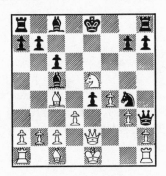

After 13. . . . N–N5

Kavalek–Ljubojevic, Amsterdam 1975.

Black has tried the attacking Schliemann Defense to the Ruy
Lopez. There is no time for normal development and consolida-
tion: White must counterattack.

14. N–B7!   . . .

A substantial improvement on the customary 14. QxP and 14.
P–Q4.

14. . . .	B–B7ch
15. K–Q1	P–K6
16. Q–B3!	. . .

The bait was 16. NxR? N–R3 17. BxP B–N5 18. BxB BxQch 19. KxB O–O–O 20. N–B7 Q–R4ch! 21. P–N4 QxPch and Black wins.

16. . . .	NxP?

Better is 16. . . . N–R3!? 17. N–Q6ch K–Q2 18. BxP Q–N5! with unclear complications.

17. Q–K4ch	K–B1
18. BxP	B–N5ch
19. K–Q2	R–K1
20. N–K5	QxP
21. BxB	QxBch
22. K–B3	. . .

Threatening 23. RxN! QxR 24. R–R1 Q–N6 25. N–N6ch PxN 26. RxR mate.

22. . . .	P–KN3
23. RxN!	QxR
24. Q–Q4	. . .

With the murderous threat of 25. NxPch PxN 26. Q–B6 mate. Black resigned after 24. . . . K–K2 25. NxB Q–K7 26. N–K5 KR–B1 27. Q–Q7ch K–B3 28. N–N4ch.

My favorite chess piece is the one that wins!
—Anonymous

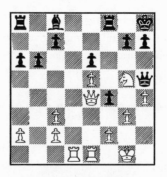

After 19. Q–K4

Rhode–Bisguier, New York 1976.

| 19. . . . | R–QN1 |

Or 19. . . . PxP 20. PxP (20. QxR? PxPch 21. K–B1 PxR=Qch 22. KxQ QxPch wins) 20. . . . R–QN1 21. R–KB1 B–N2! (22. QxB? QxR! wins).

| 20. QxP? | . . . |

Clever but not wise. 20. Q–K2 and 20. Q–B3 hold.

| 20. . . . | B–N2! |

Now the Bishop must be Black's favorite piece! Naturally not 20. . . . RxQ?? 21. R–Q8ch and mate in two.

21. Q–Q4	P–R3
22. N–K4	P–B4
23. Q–Q3	R–B6
24. Q–K2	R/1–KB1
25. N–Q2?	. . .

Relatively best is 25. R–Q3! BxN 26. QxB RxP 27. R–Q8, although Black remains better after 27. . . . Q–B2.

| 25. . . . | RxKBP! |

Very effective, but not really a Queen sacrifice.

| 26. QxR | . . . |

Practically forced, since 26. QxQ R–N7ch 27. K–R1 RxNch 28. K–N1 R–N7ch 29. K–R1 R/1–B7 (threatening both 30. . . . R–R7ch and 30. . . . RxPch) leaves Black with unstoppable mating threats.

26. . . .	RxQ
27. KxR	Q–B4ch
28. K–N1	Q–R6
Resigns	

Not caring to see 29. N–K4 BxN 30. RxB QxPch 31. K–B1 Q–B6ch and a Rook goes on the next move.

In open positions the safety of the King should be the first consideration.

—Reti

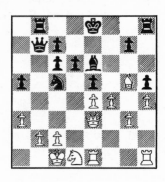

After 22. Q–K3

Dieks–Ciocaltea, Wijk aan Zee 1975.

22. . . .	N–R5!

Provoke a weakness . . .

23. P–N3	N–B4
24. PxP	BxP!!

Exploit the weakness!

25. PxP	PxP
26. P–K5	. . .

The only hope lies in a counterattack. Accepting the sacrifice loses: 26. PxB NxPch 27. K–B2 P–B4 28. Q–QB3 N–Q5ch 29. K–Q2 Q–N8! 30. Q–B4 R–N6! 31. Q–R4ch K–B2 32. Q–Q7ch K–N3 33. QxQPch K–R2.

26. . . .	BxP!
27. PxPch	. . .

If 27. KxB Q–N8ch 28. K–Q2 N–K5ch 29. K–K2 R–N6! wins.

27. . . .	N–K5

Neither King is exactly safe!

28. P–Q7ch	K–B2
29. Q–B4ch	K–N3
30. RxN	Q–N8ch
31. K–Q2	BxR

And the concluding moves were 32. Q–Q6ch K–R2 33. R–B1 R–N6! 34. Q–K5 R–Q6ch 35. K–K2 Q–B7ch. Mate next.

Three pieces are a mate.

—Eckstrom

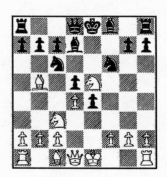

After 7. . . . B–Q2

Matvienko–Mathie, Budapest 1975.

    8. B–N5!   . . .

The fun begins with the threats of 9. BxN and 9. NxQP.

8. . . .	B–QN5
9. BxKN	QxB
10. Q–R5ch	P–N3

If 10. . . . K–K2 11. NxB KxN 12. QxPch wins.

| 11. NxB! | QxP |

If 11. . . . PxQ 12. NxQch K–B2 13. NxQP BxNch 14. NxB NxP 15. B–B4ch K–N2 16. O–O–O and White wins a Pawn.

12. Q–R3   . . .

Protecting both Knights.

12. . . .	**Q–N2**
13. Q–K6ch	**K–Q1**

If 13. . . . Q–K2 or 13. . . . N–K2 14. N–B6ch leaves White a Knight up.

14. O–O–O!   **BxN**

If 14. . . . QxN 15. Q–B6ch wins the KR.

15. RxP!	**BxPch**
16. K–N1	**N–K2**

If 16. . . . N–Q5 17. Q–B6ch QxQ 18. NxQch wins. Tactical play!

17. N–B5ch!	**NxR**
18. NxP mate!	

Combinations

"A combination is a forced variation with sacrifice," wrote Botvinnik in 1949. What distinguishes a combination from a forced maneuver, he stresses, is sacrifice. And, it may be added, sacrifice is the main difference between a combination and tactical play.

Du Mont and Spielmann lay special weight on sacrifice too. Du Mont wrote: "We are inclined, subconsciously, to rate a sacrificial combination more highly than positional play. We instinctively place the moral value above the scientific." And Spielmann concurred: "The great fascination [of a combination] is the idea of the sacrifice of material for something less tangible, but more valuable; it typifies the triumph of mind over matter." Negyesy and Hegyi, however, in their 1970 book on combinations, omit sacrifice altogether when they give the definition: "A combination is the calculation of a forcing sequence of moves which exploits, in the interest of reaching a certain aim, the special possibilities of a position." With or without a sacrifice, though, combinations deal dramatically with discovered checks, double checks, forks, skewers, pins, many kinds of sacrifices, and various types of attack. As Chernev puts it, "A combination is the heart of chess."

All very true and all very inspiring. But Lasker and Steinitz keep our feet on the ground. Lasker philosophized: "A combination must be sound. An unsound combination is no combination at all. It is merely an attempt, an error, a failure, a nonentity." And Steinitz said caustically that "A win by an unsound combination, however showy, fills me with artistic horror." A speculative combination, he discovered, and Lasker, his disciple and successor, concurred, should not be attempted in the opening and a combination should not be sought unless a player believed he held a definite advantage—an advantage in force, space, or time.

The scheme of a game is played on positional line; the decision of it, as a rule, is effected by combinations.

—Reti

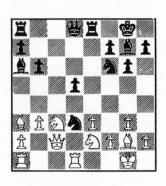

After 15. Q–B2

R. Byrne–Fischer, New York 1963–64.

15. . . .	**NxP!**

Initiating a seven-move combination.

16. KxN	**N–N5ch**
17. K–N1	**NxKP**
18. Q–Q2	**. . .**

If 19. Q–N2? QBxN wins.

18. . . .	**NxB!**

Winning the white squares.

19. KxN	**P–Q5!**
20. NxP	**B–N2ch**
21. K–B1	**. . .**

Alternatives:

A. 21. K–R3 Q–Q2ch 22. P–N4 P–KR4 wins.

B. 21. K–B2 Q–Q2! 22. QR–B1 Q–R6 23. N–B3 B–KR3 24. Q–Q3 B–K6ch 25. QxB RxQ 26. KxR R–K1ch 27. K–B2 Q–B4! winning the KN and continuing the mating attack.

C. 21. K–N1 BxNch 22. QxB R–K8ch! 23. K–B2 QxQch 24. RxQ RxR 25. R–Q7 R–QB1 26. RxB RxN 27. R–N8ch K–N2 and Black wins.

D. 21. N–B3 QxQch 22. RxQ BxN wins.

| 21. . . . | Q–Q2!! |

Resigns

Avoiding 22. Q–KB2 (22. N/4–N5 Q–R6ch 23. K–N1 B–KR3 wins) 22. . . . Q–R6ch 23. K–N1 R–K8ch!! 24. RxR BxN and wins the Queen.

Discovered Check is the dive bomber of the chessboard.

—Fine

After 22. . . . N–B4

Sasin–Korchnoi, U.S.S.R. 1973.

| 23. RxBP | . . . |

Threatening to do some dive-bombing with 24. RxNch and 25. RxQ.

| 23. . . . | R–Q8ch |
| 24. K–R2 | Q–Q3ch? |

Better chances accrue from 24. . . . N–N5ch! 25. PxN Q–Q3ch 26. Q–N3! NxQ 27. R–Q7ch K–B1 28. BxPch K–K1 29. RxQ N–B8ch 30. K–R3 RxR.

25.	P–N3	N–N5ch!
26.	K–N2!	N–R5ch!
27.	PxN	Q–R7ch
28.	K–B3	QxBPch
29.	K–K4!	. . .

On 29. KxN? Black forces mate beginning with 29. . . . R–N8ch.

29.	. . .	Q–K7ch

With a discovered check always hanging over his head, Black cannot save himself. A fantastic variation is 29. . . . R–K8ch 30. K–Q5!! N–K6ch 31. K–Q6 N–B5ch 32. QxN R–Q8ch 33. K–B7 Q–N3ch 34. K–N8 R–Q1ch 35. Q–B8 Q–Q3ch 36. R–B7ch (the dive bomber!) K–B1 37. BxPch K–K1 38. B–B7 mate!

30.	K–B4	R–B8ch
31.	K–N5	P–R3ch
32.	K–N6	. . .

Threatening 32. QxP mate and 32. Q–B8ch Q–K1 33. QxQ mate.

32.	. . .	N–K4ch
33.	QxN!	R–N8ch
34.	Q–N5!	QxB

If 34. . . . RxQch 35. PxR Q–B7ch 36. R–B5ch K–R1 37. BxP mate.

35.	RxPch	Resigns

Or 35. . . . K–B1 36. R–N8 mate.

A thorough understanding of the typical mating
continuations makes the most complicated sacrificial combinations leading up to them not only not
difficult, but almost a matter of course.

—Tarrasch

After 18. . . . RxP

Portisch–Radulov, Nice 1974.

     19. Q–R5!   . . .

With the idea of 20. NxP! KxN 21. Q–R6ch K–N1 22. B–B6 and
mate in five.

     19. . . .   **R/1–K1**

Not 19. . . . P–N3?? 20. B–B6! PxQ 21. N–R6 mate.

     20. NxP!!   . . .

A thorough understanding . . .

     20. . . .   **R/1–K4**

If 20. . . . KxN 21. Q–R6ch K–N1 22. B–B6 and mate in six.

     21. P–B4   **RxBP**
     22. N–K8!!   **Q–B3**

If 22. . . . RxN 23. BxR BxB 24. QxB wins for White.

     23. NxB   **P–B3**

If 23. . . . QxN 24. BxR RxQ 25. BxQ wins.

24. R–K1!!   **Resigns**

"A quiet move is the epitome of finesse," mused Kmoch. Black lacks an adequate way to regain his piece. For example, 24. . . . QxN 25. BxR wins. Or 24. . . . RxB 25. R–K8ch K–N2 26. R–K7ch K–B1 27. R–B7ch BxR 28. QxB mate. Or 24. . . . R–Q5 25. RxR PxR 26. N–B5 Q–K3 27. R–KB1 and White wins.

Combination is defined as two or more moves having a common object, whether offensive or defensive, and it may have place anywhere or everywhere in the game.

—Mason

After 14. BxP

Gheorghiu–Kavalek, Amsterdam 1969.

14. . . .   **NxKP!**

A surprise. But then White has not castled.

15. PxN   **RxB!!**

Two or more moves having a common object . . .

| 16. NxR | N–B5 |
| 17. Q–KB2? | . . . |

A better chance is 17. Q–Q3 NxP 18. Q–B2 NxR 19. KxN Q–R5 20. QxP.

| 17. . . . | RxP |
| 18. O–O | . . . |

The extra piece cannot be held. If 18. R–Q3 Q–K2 or . . . B–KR3 regains it.

18. . . .	NxB
19. QxPch	K–R1
20. QxBP	QxQ
21. NxQ	NxQR
22. RxN	B–Q5ch!
23. K–B1?	. . .

Loses. But after 23. K–R1 B–N5 24. R–B1 BxP the two Bishops would still win.

| 23. . . . | B–N5 |

And there followed 24. R–Q2 (24. R–K1 R–B5 mate) B–K6 25. R–QB2 R–Q5!, White resigns.

Combinations based on a double attack against the King and Queen have an elemental force.

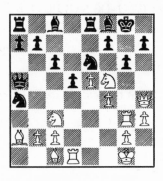

After 23. . . . N–R5

Grefe–Najdorf, Lone Pine 1976.

24. RxP!!   . . .

A tornado!

24. . . .   **Q–N3ch**

If 24. . . . PxR 25. NxP B–N2 26. N–B6ch BxN 27. QxB Q–B2 28. BxN PxB 29. N–R6 mate. Or 24. . . . PxR 25. NxP B–N2 26. N–B6ch K–B1 27. QxP PxN 28. Q–N8ch K–K2 29. QxR mate.

25. B–K3   **Q–N5**

If 25. . . . QxP? 26. N–K4! wins.

26. R–N5!!   . . .

It touches down again!

26. . . .   **NxN**

Forced. On 26. . . . PxR 27. N–Q5 Q–K8ch 28. K–R2 Black is faced with the disagreeable prospect of being mated with 29. N–B6ch K–R1 30. QxP or losing his Queen to 29. RxPch.

27. RxQ   **N–K7ch**
28. K–R2   **NxR**

29. QxN	BxR
30. N–R6ch	K–R1
31. P–B5!	N–Q1
32. PxP	BPxP
33. Q–B4!	. . .

Although Black has two Rooks for the Queen, White has a mating attack which compelled resignation after seven moves.

Deflecting maneuvers and sacrifices are the theme of many beautiful combinations.

White to move

Adams–Torre, New Orleans 1920.

1. Q–KN4!   . . .

The beginning of an attack on the eighth rank with amazing deflective sacrifices.

1. . . .   Q–N4

If 1. . . . QxQ? 2. RxRch RxR 3. RxR mate.

2. Q–QB4!   Q–Q2

Black must defend his Queen! If 2. . . . QxQ 3. RxRch RxR 4. RxR mate; if 2. . . . RxQ 3. RxRch QxR 4. RxQ mate; and if 2. . . . RxR 3. QxRch R–K1 4. RxRch QxR 5. QxQ mate.

3. Q–B7!   . . .

Again the Queen puts itself in double jeopardy.

3. . . .   Q–N4

It is mate-in-two if the Queen is captured either way. And if 3. . . . KR–Q1 4. QxQ RxQ 5. R–K8ch RxR 6. RxR mate.

4. P–QR4   QxRP

If 4. . . . QxR 5. RxQ RxQ 6. RxR mate.

5. R–K4!   Q–N4

Black must save his Queen and protect his KR at the same time. If 5. . . . RxR (5. . . . QxR 6. RxQ RxQ 7. RxR mate) 6. QxRch R–K1 7. QxRch QxQ 8. RxQ mate.

6. QxNP!   Resigns

There is no longer any way to adequately guard both the Queen and KR. A startling example of the themes of deflection and mate on the eighth.

Deflective maneuvers, sacrifices, and pins are potent weapons.

After 17. QR–K1

Braun–Matera, New York 1976.

| 17. . . . | NxN |

Setting up a pin.

| 18. BxN | B–R6! |

This wins the Exchange, but Black has something more in mind.

19. R–B2	B–Q5
20. Q–Q2	Q–K2
21. Q–K2	. . .

The potent answer to 21. P–Q6 is 21. . . . QxB! 22. RxQ RxR followed by the doubling of Rooks and mate at K8.

21. . . .	B–B4
22. B–B3	Q–Q2
23. Q–Q2	RxRch
24. QxR	R–K1
25. QxP	B–R6

Renewing the mating threats at K8.

26. P–Q6	Q–R5!
27. B–Q5ch	K–R1
28. Q–Q2	. . .

If 28. QxQ R–K8 mate.

   28. . . .   **QxRP**

Threatening 29. . . . Q–N8ch 30. Q–B1 QxQch 31. BxQ R–K8 mate. 30. . . .

   29. Q–Q1   **Q–N6!**

Shades of Adams–Torre!

   30. Q–Q2   **. . .**

If 30. QxQ R–K8 mate.

   30. . . .   **QxNP**
    Resigns

White is just about in zugzwang.

A combination is the calculation of a forcing sequence of moves which exploits, in the interest of reaching a certain aim, the special possibilities of a position.

            —Negyesy–Hegyi

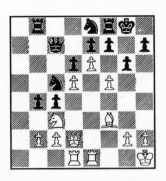

After 23. . . . P–N5

R. Weinstein–Filipowicz, Budva 1963.

24. PxPch . . .

Rather than play it safe with 24. N–K4, White starts an attack on the castled King based on a preponderance of offensive forces over defensive ones.

24. . . .	**RxP**
25. PxP	**RxB?**

Biting off too much. Necessary is 25. . . . PxP.

26. Q–R6	**PxP**

If 26. . . . N–B3 27. PxPch NxP 28. PxR wins. And if 26. . . . R–B4 27. QxPch K–B1 28. Q–R8 mate.

27. PxR	**PxN**

Black has more pieces, but they are out of play.

28. R–KN1	**P–K4**
29. RxPch	**N–N2**
30. R/1–KN1	**R–N2**
31. PxP	**P–K5**
32. PxP	**Resigns**

After 32. . . . Q–K2 33. RxNch QxR 34. RxQch RxR 35. QxP N–N2 36. Q–K6ch K–R2 37. P–K5 the connected passed pawns win easily.

Maxims of Chess

The beauty of a game of chess is usually assessed, and not without good reason, according to the sacrifices it contains.

—Spielmann

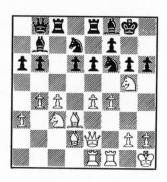

After 18. . . . P–R3

Commons–Peev, Plovdiv 1976.

19. NxBP! . . .

First, the KN is sacrificed—to breach the castled position.

19. . . . KxN
20. P–K5 N–N1

With a weak pawn formation, Black avoids the ending which results from 20. . . . PxP 21. PxP NxP 22. QxN QxQ 23. RxQ.

21. Q–N4 N–K2
22. BxPch! . . .

Second, the KB is sacrificed—to obtain the pawn break at KB5.

22. . . . NxB
23. P–KB5 N/2xP
24. PxPch!! K–K2

Or 24. . . . K–N1 25. RxN! R–K2 26. R–B7 RxR 27. PxRch KxP 28. R–B5ch K–N2 29. BxPch! KxB 30. R–B6 K–R2 31. QxNch K–R1 32. R–B7 and mates.

| 25. QxN! | K–Q1 |

Third, the Queen is "sacrificed"—for mate in two.

| 26. RxN! | . . . |

Fourth, the Exchange is sacrificed—to open the Q-file.

| 26. . . . | PxR |
| 27. BxP | RxBP |

Prolongation, though not salvation, is offered by 27. . . . Q–Q3 28. R–Q1 QxRch 29. NxQ RxBP.

| 28. QxRch! | . . . |

Fifth, and finally, the Queen is "sacrificed" again—in order to win a piece.

| 28. . . . | KxQ |
| 29. RxBch | . . . |

And after 29. . . . K–K2 30. RxQ B–B3 31. N–Q1 P–N4 32. K–N1 KxP 33. R–N6, Black resigned, being a piece behind and faced with two connected passed Pawns.

Combinations may occur at any time—in the opening, middlegame, or ending—and they may involve only a few pieces or several.

After 34. . . . R/1–R3

Izvozchikov–Elishvili, Odessa 1976.

> **35. R/B–N1!**   . . .

This saves the QRP or wins material.

> **35. . . .**   NxP
> **36. R–N5!!**   . . .

Surprisingly effective! An unclassified theme? Perhaps it might be called The Press! The threat is 37. RxR RxR 38. RxN.

> **36. . . .**   RxB

There is no way to hold the Exchange and the game. If 36. . . . RxR (36. . . . N–B6? 37. R/5xR wins) 37. BxR wins the Knight.

> **37. RxR**   . . .

And the rest is a matter of technique.

> **37. . . .**   N–B6
> **38. R–K1**   R–B2
> **39. R–K8**   R–Q2
> **40. R/5–R8**   . . .

Menacing 41. R–N8ch K–R2 42. R–R8ch K–N3 43. R/QR–N8 mate.

> **40. . . .**   P–B4
> **41. R–N8ch**   K–B3
> **42. R–R6ch**   K–K4
> **43. RxP**   . . .

And Black resigned after 43. . . . PxP 44. R–R5ch P–B4 45. PxP N–K7ch 46. K–B1 N–Q5 47. PxP NxP 48. R–KB8.

Positional Play

"Whereas by combination values are transformed, they are approved of and confirmed by 'position play.' Thus, position play is antagonistic to combination, as becomes evident when a 'combination player' meets with his counterpart, the 'position player.' The two are wholly different in makeup and constitution," philosophized Lasker. Nimzovich wrote that his conception of position play was based for the greater part on the elements he discovered and refined—the center and development, open files, the seventh and eighth ranks, the passed Pawn, exchanging, Endgame strategy, the pin, the discovered check, the Pawn chain, the doubled Pawn and restraint, the isolated Pawn, the two Bishops, overprotection, and maneuvering against weaknesses.

Steinitz, a profound thinker, was the father of positional play. The closed position, with fixed Pawns, was his special domain. He strove to convert small advantages into lasting, decisive ones. He sought to isolate hostile Pawns, create a Queenside Pawn majority, to weaken his opponent's Pawn phalanx, especially in the vicinity of the King, to obtain advance posts, and to dominate open ranks, files, and diagonals. He cultivated an assault by a Queenside chain of Pawns and went to extremes to avoid structural weaknesses when on the defense.

The process of assessing a position consists of analyzing the elements of a position, as laid down by Steinitz, Lasker, and Nimzovich, and then synthesizing those factors. The World Champions notably endowed with this remarkable positional sense are Steinitz, the primal thinker, Capablanca, whose chess was a mother tongue, Petrosian, master of restraint, Karpov, precise and determined, and Fischer. Fischer, the perfect positional player, the archetype—he is Steinitzian, Capablanca-clear, eclectic, superbly informed, rectilinear, transcendent at transitions, imaginative, and a relentless antagonist.

A rough and ready rule is that it nearly always pays to advance the front member of a doubled pawn.

—Purdy

After 7. PxB

Spassky–Fischer, Reykjavik 1972.

     7. . . .   P–Q3

Having doubled the QBPs, Black begins to operate against them in Nimzovich style.

        8. P–K4   . . .

8. N–Q2, leaving the QN1–KR7 diagonal open, may be better.

        8. . . .   **P–K4**
        9. P–Q5   **N–K2!**
       10. N–R4   **P–KR3!**

Preventing 11. B–N5.

       11. P–B4!?   . . .

Seeking the initiative. 11. P–N3 and 11. P–B3 are safer.

11. . . .	**N–N3!**

Positionally perfect—although it takes on doubled pawns and gives White a passed QP! But 11. . . . PxP? 12. BxP P–KN4 13. P–K5! N–N5 14. P–K6! N–KB3 15. O–O! and White has a winning attack.

12. NxN	**PxN**
13. PxP?	**. . .**

This presents Black with the ideal blockading square Q3. Perhaps best is 13. O–O O–O 14. P–KR3.

13. . . .	**PxP**

Why are Black's doubled Pawns better than White's? Because the placement of the pieces is such that White's can be exploited and Black's cannot.

14. B–K3	**P–N3**
15. O–O	**O–O**
16. P–QR4?	**P–QR4!**

17. P–R5 must be prevented.

17. R–N1	**B–Q2**
18. R–N2	**R–N1**
19. QR–KB2	**Q–K2**
20. B–B2	**P–KN4!**

A rough and ready rule is that . . .

21. B–Q2	**Q–K1**
22. B–K1	**Q–N3**
23. Q–Q3	**N–R4!**

Black has a positionally far superior game. The final moves were 24. RxRch RxR 25. RxRch KxR 26. B–Q1 N–B5 27. Q–B2?? BxP! White resigns. White gets mated or loses more Pawns.

The direct exploitation of an open file is sometimes impossible. But its indirect exploitation—
denial of counterplay and the opportunity to
operate in another sector—can often prove advantageous too.

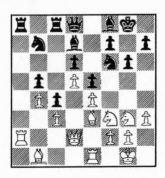

After 23. . . . Q–Q1

Karpov–Unzicker, Nice 1974.

      24. B–R7!   . . .

Thwarting Black's attempt to capture the QR-file with 24. . . .
RxR 25. BxR R–R1.

24. . . .	N–K1
25. B–B2	N–B2
26. KR–R1!	. . .

A complete reversal.

26. . . .	Q–K2
27. B–N1	B–K1
28. N–K2	. . .

Controlling the only open file, White maneuvers for a Kingside
attack. Without counterchances (only the QR-file offered any)
Black must passively await events.

28. . . .	N–Q1
29. N–R2	B–N2

| 30. P–B4 | P–B3 |

White gets the edge on 30. . . . PxP 31. QxP.

31. P–B5	P–N4
32. B–QB2	B–B2
33. N–N3	N–N2
34. B–Q1	P–R3
35. B–R5	. . .

An attack on KN6 begins.

35. . . .	Q–K1
36. Q–Q1	N–Q1
37. R–R3	K–B1
38. R/1–R2	K–N1
39. N–N4!	K–B1

Of course not 39. . . . BxB 40. NxB QxN?? 41. NxBPch BxN 42. QxQ.

40. N–K3	K–N1
41. BxBch	NxB
42. Q–R5	N–Q1
43. Q–N6!	K–B1
44. N–R5	Resigns

Zugzwang! If 44. . . . Q–K2 (the Bishop and KBP must be protected) 45. N–N4 wins a pawn. And if 44. . . . QxQ 45. PxQ N–K1 46. N–B5 (threatening 47. N/RxB NxN 48. NxQP) wins. Very positional: control of a file, restraint, play on weak squares, penetration, win of material.

The control of the center confers the possibility
of influencing activity on both wings at one and
the same time.

—Nimzovich

After 15. . . . N/3–Q2

Smyslov–Hort, Petropolis 1973.

     16. R–Q1   . . .

Putting pressure on the half-open center file. Threat: 17. P–N4
N–N6 18. N/4–K2 P–Q4 19. PxN BxQNP 20. R–B1 and White is
a piece up.

16. . . .	**N–N1**
17. B–K3	**N–B3**
18. Q–N3	. . .

In the style of Yates, long ago. White stands better.

18. . . .	**KR–K1**
19. B–N2	**B–B1**
20. R–B2	**Q–Q2**
21. N–B3	**N–N5**
22. N–K5	. . .

Activity on the right wing begins.

22. . . .	**Q–B2**
23. N–N4	**N–Q2**
24. B–Q4!	. . .

Threatening 25. N–R6ch K–R1 (25. . . . PxN allows mate in two)
26. NxPch K–N1 27. N–R6ch K–R1 28. P–N6 and wins.

24. . . .	P–K4
25. PxP	NxKP
26. R/1–KB1	R–K2?

"Without error there can be no brilliancy."—Lasker. Best is 26.
. . . NxN 27. QxN R–K2, but 28. P–R4 keeps the attack.

27. BxN	PxB
28. N–B6ch!	K–R1
29. NxP!	R–K3

If 29. . . . KxN 30. P–N6ch PxP 31. RxB RxR 32. RxR soon mates.

30. RxP	B–B4ch
31. K–R1	R–K2
32. R–B8ch	Resigns

Or 32. . . . RxR 33. RxRch KxN 34. P–N6ch K–R3 35. R–R8 mate.

One of the most important types of attack on the castled King on the KR-file is that which involves the doubling of the heavy pieces on the file, threatening mate at KR8.

—Vukovic

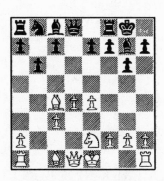

After 8. . . . P–N3

Petrosian–Stean, Moscow 1975.

9. P–KR4!   . . .

Commencing the attack on the KR-file.

9. . . .	N–B3
10. P–R5	N–R4
11. B–Q3	P–K4

With White boasting a quantitative and qualitative central Pawn majority, Black's attempt to find counterplay in the center is bound to fail.

12. RPxP   RPxP

Avoiding 12. . . . KPxP? 13. PxRPch K–R1 14. B–KR6 PxP 15. BxBch KxB 16. Q–B1! Q–B3 17. P–K5! Q–K3 18. P–R8=Qch RxQ 19. Q–N5ch Q–N3 20. BxQ RxRch 21. N–N1 RxNch 22. K–K2 RxR 23. Q–B6ch K–R3 24. BxPch K–R2 25. Q–N6ch K–R1 26. Q–R6 mate.

13. B–KR6	P–KB3
14. Q–Q2	Q–K2
15. O–O–O	B–K3
16. P–Q5	B–Q2
17. R–R2	R–B2
18. R/1–R1!	. . .

Doubling the heavy pieces and threatening 19. BxB KxB (19. . . . RxB 20. R–R8ch K–B2 21. RxR wins) 20. R–R7ch K–B1 21. R–R8ch K–N2 22. R/1–R7 mate.

18. . . .	R–K1
19. P–KB4	P–B3
20. PxKP	QxP
21. N–B4	P–KN4
22. N–N6	Q–Q3
23. BxB	RxB

If 23. . . . KxB 24. R–R7ch K–N1 25. R–R8ch K–N2 26. R/1–R7ch KxN 27. P–K5ch wins the Queen.

24. P–K5!	RxP

If 24. . . . PxP 25. R–R8ch K–B2 26. R–B1ch wins.

25. PxP	BxP
26. NxR	QxN
27. R–R8ch	K–B2
28. R–B1	B–K5
29. Q–K1	Resigns

For if 29. . . . P–B4 30. BxB leaves White a Rook ahead.

The passed pawn should be advanced when it is likely to reach its queening goal.

—Nimzovich

After 14. . . . N–R5

R. Byrne–Smyslov, Biel 1976.

15. P–B4	. . .

This pawn has a bright future. Threat: 16. P–B5, opening the KB-file.

15. . . .	N–KB4

If 15. . . . P–KN3 16. P–B5!? NxKBP 17. NxN NPxN 18. P–N4, PxP 19. BxP and White's pieces penetrate the Kingside.

16. NxN	PxN
17. P–N4!	PxP
18. BxP	P–B4

Or 18. . . . O–O–O 19. P–B5 QR–K1 20. R–K1 and White breaks through with P–K6.

19. PxP e.p.	O–O–O

If 19. . . . PxP? 20. R–K1ch K–Q1 21. BxB KxB 22. Q–N4ch and White has a winning King-hunt going.

20. PxP	KR–N1
21. K–R1	RxP
22. BxBch	R/1xB
23. P–B5	Q–Q1

Black must reorganize to stop the passed Pawn.

24. Q–B3	N–N3
25. B–B4	R/Q–KB2
26. B–N3!	. . .

Threatening 27. Q–B4 N–Q2 28. Q–Q6 Q–R4 29. QR–K1.

26. . . .	Q–N4
27. QR–K1	Q–N5
28. Q–K3	R–K2

Mate must be prevented. If 28. . . . Q–K5ch 29. QxQ PxQ 30. RxP and White wins with his two extra pawns.

29. QxR!	. . .

To demonstrate the power of the passed Pawn.

29. . . .	RxQ
30. RxR	K–Q1
31. P–B6	. . .

Threatening 32. P–B7 KxR 33. P–B8=Qch and mate in two.

31. . . .	N–Q2
32. RxNch!	KxR
33. P–B7	. . .

Reaching for its goal. The rest was 33. . . . Q–K5ch 34. K–N1 Q–K6ch 35. K–N2 Q–K5ch 36. R–B3 QxPch 37. K–R3, Black resigns.

Weak points or holes in the opponent's position must be occupied by pieces, not pawns.
—Tarrasch

After 29. . . . P–QR4

Browne–Timman, Amsterdam 1976.

30. P–B5 . . .

White ties together two positional themes, the occupation of weak points and the conversion of a Pawn majority into a passed Pawn.

30. . . . **NPxP**

Missing the opportunity to liquidate the dominating Knight with 30. . . . RPxP 31. BPxP R/2–Q2 32. PxP NxKP! 33. RxN RxN.

31. PxBP	**N–N1**
32. R–QB3	**R–B3**

Not 32. . . . N–Q2 33. P–B6 NxP? 34. N–N5 and White wins a piece.

| 33. R–Q2 | N–R3 |

And if 33. . . . N–Q2 34. N–N7 wins a piece.

34. R/2–QB2	R–Q2
35. K–B2	R/2–B2
36. N–K4	R–B1
37. K–K3	R–N1
38. R–Q2	N–B2
39. N–B6ch	. . .

Like Q6 and QN6, this hole is ideal for a piece.

| 39. . . . | K–N2 |
| 40. R–Q6 | . . . |

To remove one of the blockaders.

40. . . .	N–N4
41. RxR	NxR
42. R–N6	R–Q1
43. R–Q6	R–QB1
44. P–B6!	. . .

A little combination which involves a temporary Exchange sacrifice.

| 44. . . . | P–N4 |

If 44. . . . N–N4 45. P–QR4 NxR 46. PxN RxP (46. . . . KxN 47. P–B7 followed by 48. P–Q7 wins) 47. P–Q7 R–Q3 48. N–K8ch wins.

| 45. K–Q4 | N–R5 |
| 46. P–B7 | K–N3 |

If 46. . . . RxP 47. N–K8ch wins the Rook.

| 47. N–K8! | Resigns |

With 48. R–Q8 coming, Black had no alternative.

The Queen-side attack in the middle game, often based on a pawn-majority, is local, violent, and aims at definite objects.

—Euwe

After 20. K–N1

Quinteros–Larsen, Manila 1973.

    20. . . .   **N–R4!**

Black spots the holes at QB5 and QN6 and frees his QBP.

    21. Q–Q3   **N–B5**
    22. B–Q2   **PxP!**
    23. QPxP   **. . .**

If 23. BPxP Q–N5! But now Black has a massive Queenside Pawn roller.

    23. . . .   **QR–Q1**
    24. B–B1   **P–QN4**
    25. KR–K1   **KR–K1**

Restraining both the KP and BP.

    26. Q–KB3   **P–B4**
    27. R–Q3   **P–Q5**
    28. R/1–Q1   **N–R4**

Heading for the other hole and again freeing the QBP.

| 29. P–KN4 | N–N6 |

Threatening to win the Exchange with 30. . . . P–B5.

| 30. R–K1 | . . . |

30. RxN PxR 31. QxPch P–B5 32. Q–KB3 P–Q6 leaves Black with a winning material and positional advantage.

| 30. . . . | P–B5 |
| 31. R/3–Q1 | P–N5! |

A thematic, effective Pawn breakthrough.

| 32. PxP | P–Q6 |
| 33. B–Q2 | P–R6! |

Securing two connected passed Pawns.

34. PxP	N–Q5
35. Q–B2	Q–R5
36. B–B3	N–K7
37. B–N2	Q–B7ch
Resigns	

Else a Rook drops with 38. K–R1 P–B6 39. B–B1 N–Q5! 40. QxQ NxQch 41. K–R2 NxR 42. RxN P–Q7 43. R–Q1 PxB=Q 44. RxQ R–Q6.

A powerful center can be used to create a King-side attack.

—Byrne

After 7. . . . B–N5

N. Weinstein–Lein, New York 1976.

8. P–K5 . . .

The QP is preserved and the broad Pawn center begins to make itself felt.

8. . . .	PxP
9. QPxP	N–Q4
10. P–KR3!	. . .

With an eye to controlling the center, White willingly takes on doubled QBPs.

10. . . .	NxN
11. PxN	B–B4
12. B–K3	BxB

Due to a lack of space, Black already cannot find a good move. If 12. . . . Q–Q2, 13. N–Q4 BxB 14. PxB improves White's position. And if 12. . . . P–B3, 13. BxB PxB 14. Q–K2 PxP 15. Q–B4ch K–R1 16. N–N5 and White wins the Exchange.

13. PxB . . .

Now the Pawns are restraightened and ready to advance.

13. . . .	P–N3
14. Q–K2	N–R4
15. P–Q4	Q–Q2

If 15. . . . Q–Q4, 16. N–Q2 P–QN4 17. P–B5 affords White a good Kingside initiative.

| 16. P–B4 | QR–Q1 |
| 17. QR–B1 | P–KB3 |

Somewhat better is 17. . . . P–QB3, but there is no real defense against the advancing Pawns.

18. P–Q5	P–B3
19. KR–Q1	Q–N2
20. N–Q4	R–Q2
21. N–K6	. . .

An ideal outpost.

| 21. . . . | R–B1 |
| 22. P–KB5! | . . . |

Going over to the Kingside attack.

| 22. . . . | NPxP |
| 23. Q–B3 | . . . |

Menacing 24. Q–N3.

23. . . .	B–R1
24. QxP	QBPxP
25. R–Q4!	Resigns

It is finished. If 25. . . . RxP 26. R/1xR NxR 27. R–N4ch K–B2 28. N–Q8ch! RxN 29. P–K6ch K–B1 30. QxRP and mates.

The main objective of any operation in an open file is the eventual occupation of the seventh or eighth rank.

—Nimzovich

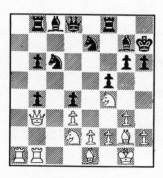

After 19. . . . P–N5

D. Byrne–Evans, San Antonio 1972.

20. N–K6	. . .

Infiltration on the white squares is begun with the winning of the minor Exchange.

20. . . .	BxN
21. QxB	R–B3
22. Q–N3	B–B1
23. N–B1	N–B1

White regains the pawn sacrificed earlier in the game.

24. BxN	RxB
25. BxP	B–N2

The ending reached with 25. . . . BxB 26. QxB R–B7 27. R–N2 RxR 28. QxR distinctly favors White.

26. R–B1	N–R2

Preferable, though less witty, is 26. . . . RxR.

27. Q–B7!	. . .

Occupation of the seventh rank. Of course if 27. RxN? RxR.

27. . . .	RxR
28. RxR	N–N4
29. R–B6	Q–N4

After 29. . . . Q–K1 30. QxQ RxQ 31. RxQNP N–B6 32. P–K3 PxP 33. PxP White wins the ending.

30. N–Q2!	R–QR1
31. N–B3	Q–R4
32. RxQNP	N–B6
33. NxP	Resigns

Since 33. . . . NxPch 34. NxN QxN 35. B–B3 R–KN1 36. QxPch K–R1 37. QxRP mates.

Over-protection of the strong point K5 affords security to the point and affords a source of energy to the protectors.

—Nimzovich

After 16. . . . N–B4

R. Weinstein–Turner, New York 1961–62.

17. N–Q6   . . .

The strong point at K5 provides a source of energy to the protector.

17. . . .	P–Q6
18. BxP	NxB
19. QxN	BxN
20. N–N5!	. . .

An effective zwischenzug: more energy for another protector.

20. . . .	P–N3
21. PxB	. . .

Roles change: the strong point becomes a passed pawn.

21. . . .	Q–R4
22. Q–KR3	. . .

The mate threats improve the position of the White pieces and force weaknesses in Black's castled setup.

22. . . .	P–R4
23. N–K4	N–N1
24. N–B6ch	K–N2
25. P–Q7!	. . .

An example of "the passed Pawn's lust to expand."

25. . . .	N–B3

If 25. . . . KxN? 26. P–Q8=Qch RxQ 27. RxR QxR 28. Q–R4ch wins the Black Queen.

26. N–K8ch	KRxN

Confronted by the imminent infiltration of the White men on the dark squares, Black is practically obliged to sacrifice the Exchange.

27. PxR=Q	RxQ
28. R–Q7	B–B1
29. R–B7	N–Q5
30. Q–K3	P–K4

Or 30. . . . N–B4 31. Q–K5ch QxQ 32. BxQch K–N1 33. QR–QB1 N–K2 34. B–Q6 and White wins the Bishop.

31. RxB!   **Resigns**

If 31. . . . RxR 32. BxPch wins the Knight.

Exchanging

Exchanging is one of the basic elements of Chess. And yet it is the most neglected subject in the vast literature on the game! Only Nimzovich (*My System*, "On Exchanging," six pages), Pachman (*Modern Chess Strategy*, "Exchange of Material," six pages), and Locock (*100 Chess Maxims*, "Exchanging," one page in a twenty-seven-page booklet!) devote a chapter to it!

Exchanging is not only the means by which Openings are turned into Middlegames, and Middlegames into Endgames, it is also a device by which one type of Opening is changed into another, one Middlegame into another, and one Endgame changed into another. Nimzovich explains that exchanges are made in order to seize an open file, to destroy a defending piece, to avoid losing time by retreating, to exploit a material advantage, to work on an open file, and to eliminate weak Pawns and squares. Pachman lists four cases in which exchanges are advantageous: when an inactive piece is exchanged for an active one; when an exchange prevents the opponent from defending a weak point; when an exchange makes it easier to convert a material or positional superiority into a win, or makes it harder for the opponent to do so; and when an exchange lightens the defense or lessens the effect of an opponent's spatial advantage. And Locock says: "**Exchange is not loss. Beginners usually think it is. Remember that after the exchange *it is still your move*.**"

Timid, draw-seeking, mechanical, thoughtless exchanges are unrewarding and esthetically abhorrent. It is the converse— Capablanca's deliberate, early exchange of Queens, Petrosian's catlike stalking of the Ending, and Fischer's precise transitions— which makes exchanging an important, exciting, basic element of chess.

Every important exchange of material alters in some way the character of the position and necessitates a change in the strategical and, tactical conduct of the game.

—Pachman

After 21. . . . B–Q2

Fischer–Petrosian, Buenos Aires 1971.

22. NxBch!   . . .

Having already judiciously exchanged the Queens and a pair of Bishops and Knights, White now exchanges to obtain a Bishop which is much superior to the Knight and to maintain control of the open files with his Rooks.

22. . . .	**RxN**
23. R–QB1	**R–Q3**

If 23. . . . P–N3 (White threatened 24. BxQRP) 24. R–B6 and Black's QRP falls.

24. R–B7   . . .

Threatening to win with 25. R/5–K7.

24. . . .	**N–Q2**
25. R–K2	**P–N3**
26. K–B2	**P–KR4**

What else? If 26. . . . R–K1 27. RxRch KxR 28. R–R7 R–N3 29. P–QR3 N–N1 30. K–K3 P–R3 31. K–Q4 N–B3ch 32. K–B5 NxR 33. KxR N–B1ch 34. K–B7 N–K2 35. BxRP and White has a simple win.

27.	P–B4	P–R5
28.	K–B3	P–B4

Weak but forced since 29. K–N4 had to be stopped.

29.	K–K3	P–Q5ch
30.	K–Q2	. . .

The intention is to liquidate the QP with 31. B–B4, 32. K–Q3, and 33. R–K6.

30.	. . .	N–N3
31.	R/2–K7	N–Q4
32.	R–B7ch	K–K1
33.	R–QN7	NxBP

There is no defense to the threat of 34. R–KR7. On 33. . . . R–N3 34. RxR NxR (34. . . . KxR 35. B–B4 wins) 35. R–KN7 K–B1 36. RxP N–Q4 37. B–B4 wins more material.

34.	B–B4	Resigns

Black is in a mating net. On 34. . . . N–Q4 (34. . . . N–K3 35. R/N–K7ch wins the Knight) 35. BxN RxB 36. R–KR7 forces mate.

Capablanca can be regarded as the great master of simplification.

—Euwe

After 22. . . . N–B3

Capablanca–L. Steiner, Budapest 1928.

23. RxB!   . . .

White selects a simple, forcing, exchanging course to enter a winning ending.

23. . . .   NxN

Of course if 23. . . . RxR?? 24. QxN wins two pieces for a Rook.

24. RxR   RxR
25. B–K2!   Q–Q7

Black must exchange Queens perforce. On 25. . . . N–Q2 (25. . . . N–Q6 26. R–Q1 wins the Knight) 26. R–Q1 Q–K2 (26. . . . Q–N1 27. Q–Q2! maintains the winning pin) 27. Q–B7 K–B1 28. B–N5 K–K1 29. RxN! RxR 30. Q–B8ch Q–Q1 31. BxRch White is a Bishop ahead.

26. QxQ!   . . .

The nod goes to another simple exchange. 26. PxN QxPch 27. K–R1 R–Q7 28. Q–B8ch K–N2 29. B–B3 wins a piece but affords Black a little counterplay and the chance for longer resistance.

26. . . .	RxQ
27. R–B8ch	K–N2
28. K–B1!	N–Q2

Or 28. . . . N–Q6 29. R–Q8 and wins.

| 29. R–Q8 | K–B3 |
| 30. B–N5 | R–Q4 |

White obtains a won King-and-Pawn ending on 30. . . . K–K2 31. RxNch RxR 32. BxR KxB 33. P–QR4!

31. P–QR4! . . .

Quickest and clearest. If 31. BxN K–K2 32. R–QN8 RxB 33. RxP R–R2 34. P–N5 RxP.

31. . . . RxB

Fatalism. But, again, if 31. . . . K–K2 then White exchanges all the pieces and wins the King-and-Pawn Ending.

| 32. PxR | K–K2 |
| 33. R–QB8! | . . . |

And the remainder was 33. . . . P–K4 34. R–B6! P–K5 35. K–K2 P–B4 36. K–Q2 K–B2 37. K–B3, Black resigns.

If a won ending is on the Horizon, the guiding principle is to simplify the position by exchanges.

After 25. ... B–Q2

Botvinnik–Boleslavsky, Moscow 1941.

26. NxB	. . .

A Pawn is garnered and the exchanges begin.

26. . . .	**RxN**

Not 26. ... NxN?? 27. RxRch RxR 28. RxR mate.

27. QxP	. . .

The weakness of the last rank shows.

27. . . .	**Q–Q1**

If 27. ... QxP 28. QxR NxQ 29. RxR mate, and if 27. ... NxQ 28. RxR mate.

28. N–B3	**R–QB2?**
29. NxN!	**PxN**

Alternatives: a) 29. ... RxQ 30. N–B7ch K–N1 31. NxQ RxN 32. P–B4 P–B4 33. R–B4 P–N4 34. RxP RxP 35. RxPch K–R1 36. P–N5 wins; and b) 29. ... RxN 30. RxR PxR (30. ... RxQ? 31. R–K8ch QxR 32. RxQ mate) 31. Q–K4 and the two connected passed Pawns decide.

30. QxRch!	. . .

Indomitably exchanging.

30. . . .	**QxQ**
31. RxP	**Q–KN1**

Due to the vulnerability of his first rank, there is no way to save the Queen.

32. R–K8	**RxP**
33. RxQch	**KxR**
34. R–QN1	. . .

White has a won Rook-and-Pawn Endgame. A *BCE* win. Simplifying exchanges, embodying pretty combinations, extracted it from an unclear, complicated Middlegame. Still, it required thirty-one more moves of logical, precise Endgame play for White to chalk up the point: 34. . . . K–B2 35. P–N5 K–K3 36. P–N6 R–B1 37. P–R3! R–QN1 38. K–R2 K–Q4 39. K–N3 K–B3 40. K–N4 K–N2 41. R–K1!! R–N1 42. R–K6 K–R3 43. K–N5 K–N2 44. P–R4 K–R3 45. P–R5 K–N2 46. P–N4 K–R3 47. K–R4 K–N2 48. P–R6! PxP 49. RxP R–N2 50. K–R5 K–R3 51. R–QB6! R–K2 52. R–B7 R–K4ch 53. P–N5 KxP 54. RxP K–B3 55. K–R6 K–Q3 56. P–N6 R–K8 57. R–KB7 K–K3 58. R–B2 R–R8 59. P–N7 R–R8ch 60. K–N6 R–N8ch 61. K–R7 R–R8ch 62. K–N8 K–K2 63. R–K2ch K–Q2 64. R–K4! R–R7 65. K–B7, Black resigns.

An exchange of pieces is advantageous when it prevents the opponent from effectively defending weak points in his position.

—Pachman

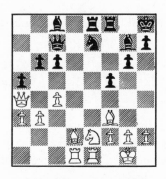

After 28. . . . N–K2

Schmidt–Smyslov, Amsterdam 1954.

      29. P–B5!   . . .

An exchange of pawns, cracking Black's Queenside formation, foreshadows the exchange of additional pawns and several pieces.

29. . . .	**PxP**
30. QxRP	**Q–N1**

After 30. . . . QxQ 31. BxQ, the doubled pawns soon fall.

31. QxP	**QxP**
32. N–Q4	**Q–N2**

Forced, since 32. . . . BxN? 33. QxBch K–N1 34. B–B3 wins at once for White.

      33. NxQBP   . . .

Wins a pawn and forces more exchanges.

33. . . .	**NxN**
34. BxN	**RxRch**
35. RxR	**Q–N7**

If 35. . . . Q–QB2 36. QxRch! BxQ 37. B–B3ch Q–N2 (if 37. . . .
K–N1 38. B–Q5ch wins, and if 37. . . . B–N2 38. R–K8 mate) 38.
BxQch KxB 39. R–K8 B–R3 40. P–QR4 wins.

36. B–B4   **R–Q1**

Or 36. . . . Q–B3 37. B–K5 Q–B2 38. B–Q5 and White wins.

37. Q–K7   **Q–Q5**

If 37. . . . Q–B3 38. Q–QB7, threatening 39. B–K5, wins.

38. Q–K8ch!   . . .

A dramatic example of the exchanging device.

38. . . .   **RxQ**

If 38. . . . B–B1 39. B–K5ch wins.

39. RxRch   **B–B1**
40. B–K5ch   **QxB**
41. RxQ   **Resigns**

Exchanging pieces and pawns to open a vital diagonal is a deadly device.

After 13. . . . O–O

Nimzovich–Behting, Riga 1919.

14. P–B4   . . .

With the intention of 15. P–KB5 B–Q2 16. PxP PxP 17. NxKP! NxN? 18. BxP winning the Queen.

14. . . .   PxP
15. N/2xBP   . . .

Threatening 16. N–Q6 Q–K2 17. BxBch QxB 18. NxNP.

15. . . .   Q–K2
16. P–B5   B–Q4

In order to hold Q4 and overprotect the KP.

17. NxB   . . .

Exchanging wins the minor Exchange.

17. . . .   PxN
18. N–K3   . . .

A new blockader, which obstructs the KP, holds the BP, and attacks the QP.

18. . . .   Q–Q2
19. NxP!!   . . .

Apparently a sacrifice, this is actually a way to exchange material and open the QR2–KN8 diagonal.

19. . . .   NxN
20. QxP   R–Q1
21. P–B6!   . . .

Menacing 22. P–B7ch K–B1 23. QxP or 22. R–B5, regaining the piece.

21. . . .   PxP

No defense. If 21. . . . N–B3 22. P–B7ch K–R1 23. BxN gives White a winning material and positional game (23. . . . QxB? 24. QxQ RxQ 25. P–B8=Qch RxQ 26. RxR mate). Or if 21. . . . N–B3

22. P–B7ch K–B1 23. BxN QxB 24. QxP QxPch 25. K–R1 N–K4 26.
Q–N8ch K–K2 27. P–B8=Qch RxQ 28. QxPch wins.

22. R–B5	K–R1
23. RxN	. . .

Exchange completed.

23. . . .	R–K1

If 23. . . . Q–K1? 24. B–B2! wins a whole Rook.

24. RxQ	RxQ
25. R–Q8ch	K–N2
26. R–N8ch	K–R3
27. R–KB1	Resigns

Black loses his QR or gets mated.

**A player with two minor pieces for a Rook and
two pawns should avoid exchanging Queens.**

After 34. . . . B–N4

R. Byrne–Liberzon, Haifa 1976.

35. BxPch!	. . .

White avoids exchanging his Queen in order to preserve mating threats with it and minor pieces. After 35. QxPch? QxQ 36. BxQch K–B1 (threatening 37. . . . R–Q1) Black's Endgame prospects are bright.

35. . . .		K–R1
36.	Q–KB3	Q–B3
37.	N–KB5!	. . .

Again, avoiding an exchange of Queens, even though it means enduring a pin.

37. . . .		R–KB1
38.	N/3–Q4	B–Q2

Intending to swap at least a pair of minor pieces.

39.	B–K4	BxN
40.	NxB	Q–R8
41.	Q–K3	B–Q5
42.	NxB	. . .

Black hoped for 42. QxBch? QxQ 43. NxQ R–B8ch 44. K–N2 RxB with the better chances.

42. . . .		R–B8ch
43.	K–N2	QxB

If 43. . . . RxB? 44. Q–B2 RxB 45. Q–B8ch K–R2 46. Q–B5ch K–N2 47. QxR and White wins.

44.	N–K2!	. . .

Still maintaining the Queens.

44. . . .		R–B3

Attempting to safeguard the King and third-rank Pawns. On 44. . . . R–N8ch 45. K–R2! R–B8 46. Q–Q4ch White penetrates with his Queen and Bishop, wins a pawn or two, regroups around his King, and goes on to win with a Queenside Pawn advance or a direct attack on the King.

45.	B–B3	Q–R8
46.	N–Q4	Q–R7ch

47. K–N3	K–N2
48. Q–K7ch	Q–B2

If 48. . . . R–B2 49. N–K6ch wins.

49. Q–K5!	P–KR4

After 49. . . . K–R1 50. B–Q5 Q–KN2 51. N–B5 Q–B1 52. N–K7 K–R2 53. B–K4ch K–N2 54. K–N2 K–B2 55. B–Q5ch K–N2 56. N–N8 White wins the Exchange and game.

50. B–Q5	Resigns

For if 50. . . . Q–N3 51. N–K6ch K–R3 52. B–K4 RxN (52. . . . Q–B2 53. QxP mate) 53. Q–R8ch Q–R2 54. QxQ mate.

The process for carrying out the transition to a favorable ending is characterized by restraint, compulsion, threats, and maneuvers which can be warded off only by exchanges.

—Reinfeld

After 18. R–B3

L. Portisch–Sanguinetti, Biel 1976.

18. . . .   N–K5!

Compelling the exchange of two pairs of minor pieces by threatening the Queen and Knight/B4.

19.	BxN	PxB
20.	NxNch	QxN
21.	R/3–B1	P–B3
22.	N–N4	B–Q4
23.	P–B5	P–N5

The exchanges have blunted White's Kingside initiative and sharpened Black's advance with the Queenside Pawn majority.

24.	N–B2	KR–B1
25.	PxP	PxP
26.	RxR	RxR

Further exchanges, induced by the desire to keep a Rook on the Kingside, have given Black control of the only open file.

27. N–R3   . . .

The idea behind this is to construct a dominating center with 28. N–B4 B–B2 29. P–Q5 followed by 30. Q–Q4 and 31. N–K6.

27. . . .   P–B6!

But Black comes first with a brilliant sacrifice which obtains a passed Pawn and activates all the Black pieces.

28.	PxP	R–R7
29.	Q–B1	P–N6!

A little giant.

30. P–B4   . . .

A desperate attempt to find play for the Queen.

30.	. . .	R–QB7
31.	Q–R1	BxP
32.	Q–R8ch	Q–B1
33.	Q–R4	. . .

If 33. QxQch KxQ 34. R–N1 P–N7 wins.

33. . . .	**Q–B1**

Stronger than winning the Exchange with 33. . . . BxR 34. QxPch R–B5 35. KxB Q–B1.

34. R–N1	**K–R1!**
35. N–B4	**B–N1**

Threatening 36. . . . R–B8ch 37. RxR QxRch 38. K–B2 P–N7.

36. R–KB1	**Q–B6**
Resigns	

Black threatens not only to promote the QNP but also to win a piece with 37. . . . QxPch 38. K–R1 QxN (39. RxQ R–B8ch 40. R–B1 RxR mate).

Many attacks succeed because the attacker forces the exchange of his opponent's best defensive pieces.

—Byrne

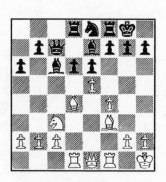

After 15. . . . R–Q1

Geller–Sigurjonsson, Wijk aan Zee 1976.

| 16. R–Q3 | . . . |

With the intention of switching the Rook to a Kingside file.

| 16. . . . | PxP |
| 17. PxP | P–KN3 |

Unfortunately for him, Black does not have the option of ex-changing a pair of Rooks and two pairs of Bishops; e.g., 17. . . . BxB 18. R/1xB B–B4? 19. BxB RxR 20. BxR RxR 21. B–Q6! NxB 22. PxN Q–B3 23. PxR QxPch 24. K–N1 Q–N5ch 25. Q–N3 and White remains a Knight ahead.

18. Q–B2	R–Q2
19. BxB	QxB
20. R–B3	Q–B5!
21. B–K3!	. . .

Refusing to fall into the trap 21. RxP?? QxRch!! 22. QxQ RxR 23. Q–KN1 RxB! 24. QxR R–B8ch 25. Q–N1 RxQch, and Black emerges with an extra Bishop.

21. . . .	B–R5
22. Q–N1	B–Q1
23. B–B5!	. . .

Forcing the exchange of Bishops, preparing to exploit the hole at KB6, and dramatizing the difference in the effectiveness of the two Knights.

23. . . .	B–K2
24. BxB	RxB
25. Q–K3	N–N2
26. P–QN3	Q–B2
27. N–K4!	N–B4

If 27. . . . QxKP? 28. N–B6ch wins the Queen; and if 27. . . . QxBP? 28. N–B6ch K–R1 29. Q–R6 forces mate.

| 28. N–B6ch | K–N2 |

If 28. . . . K–R1 29. RxN KPxR 30. Q–R6 forces mate.

29. R–R3!   **Resigns**

No one likes to be checkmated. If 29. . . . R–KR1 (29. . . . NxQ 30. RxP mate) 30. RxN! KPxR 31. Q–R6 mate. And if 29. . . . P–KR4 30. NxPch! PxN 31. Q–N5ch K–R2 32. RxPch N–R3 33. RxN mate.

If you have an advantage in material, the guiding line is to simplify the position by exchanges.

—Euwe

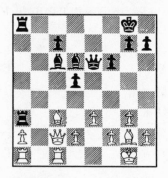

After 21. . . . B–Q3

Denker–Steiner, New York 1946.

22. B–N4!   . . .

A Pawn up, ergo, exchange!

22. . . .   **R/6–R3**

Or 22. . . . BxB (22. . . . B–R5 23. Q–N2) 23. QxB QxQ 24. RxQ R–Q1 (24. . . . BxP 25. BxPch wins) 25. P–Q4 R–R2 26. R–N1 B–B1 27. R–N5 and White wins the QP.

23. Q–N3!   . . .

Threatening to win the Queen with 24. RxB! RxR 25. BxP, and, at the same time, simplifying the position by exchanges.

| 23. . . . | BxB |
| 24. RxB! | Q–K2 |

Not 24. . . . QxR?? or 24. . . . RxR?? 25. BxP(ch) winning the Queen.

| 25. BxPch | K–R1 |
| 26. RxQBP! | . . . |

Combinative exchanges!

26. . . .	QxR
27. BxR	BxP
28. B–Q5	. . .

Taking an iron grip on the passed pawn and preparing to exploit the two-pawn plus.

28. . . .	P–N3
29. Q–Q3	Q–R4
30. Q–K4	. . .

Threatening 31. Q–K7.

| 30. . . . | Q–Q1 |
| 31. R–Q1 | Q–B2? |

Hoping for 32. RxB? Q–B8ch 33. K–N2 QxR, but this loses the Bishop. However, the alternative 31. . . . B–R4 32. B–N3 loses too.

| 32. Q–Q3 | Resigns |

Black cannot defend both the Rook and Bishop.

In many opening systems an important part is played by simplification which leads quickly to a complicated endgame position.

—Suetin

After 11. P–KN3

Chistyakov–Suetin, Riga 1954.

| 11. . . . | BxNch! |

An important, simplifying exchange. White's Queenside Pawns are split and the loss of the minor Exchange is not significant.

| 12. PxB | N–B3 |
| 13. B–N2 | K–B1 |

Black has been deprived of the castling privilege, but this too is not significant.

14. O–O	R–Q1
15. P–QR4	B–Q4
16. B–R3ch	. . .

Better is 16. BxB RxB 17. KR–Q1.

16. . . .	P–K3
17. P–B3	B–B5
18. K–B2	P–N3
19. KR–Q1	K–N2
20. B–N5	R–Q4!

Refusing to cede the file.

21.	RxR	PxR
22.	R–Q1	R–K1
23.	R–K1	N–N1!

With an eye on the weak QRP.

24.	P–K4?	. . .

Taking on a third isolated Pawn. Preferable is 24. P–K3.

24.	. . .	PxP
25.	PxP	B–K3!

Of course 25. . . . RxP?? 26. B–N2 costs the Exchange.

26.	B–KB1	. . .

After 26. BxB RxB 27. R–Q8 P–B3! 28. B–B4 N–B3 29. R–Q7ch K–R3 30. RxP RxP 31. R–KB7 R–K3! Black threatens to win the QRP and QBP.

26.	. . .	R–QB1
27.	B–B6	N–Q2
28.	B–Q4	N–B4!

And Black exploited the weak Pawns to win the Endgame.

Strategy

Strategy is a plan or technique for achieving some end, the ideas which lie behind a player's moves and which guide his thinking during the game. It is everything one does, from deciding between 1. P–K4 and 1. P–Q4 to deciding whether to play for mate or for the win of a Pawn. Chess is a game of strategy.

A variety of stratagems are shown in the following pages: Fischer exchanges a bad Bishop for a good one and mounts a Kingside attack, Botvinnik elects to win the Endgame with a Queenside Pawn advance, Reshevsky relies on a passed QBP, Bogolyubov shifts his attack from one sector to another, Evans creates a dominating central position, Bisguier exploits a weak pawn structure, Kavalek banks on a mating attack, Mednis sacrifices pieces, Fuderer punishes pawn grabbing, and Rogoff returns extra material to accomplish a favorable transition. The ways of strategy are many and devious.

Nimzovich regarded the center, play in open files, play on the seventh and eighth ranks, the passed Pawn, the pin, discovered check, exchanging, and the pawn chain as the elements of chess strategy. To this must be added other positional characteristics: material superiority or equality, mobility of the pieces, the strength or weakness of an individual Pawn, the over-all pawn structure, cooperation of all the Pawns and pieces, and King safety. And, finally, there is always the worrisome question: "What is the threat?"

Based on these elements and characteristics and with that question in mind, the master forms his judgment, makes his plan, and sets his strategy.

In Fischer's games it is easier to explain the strategical backbone than in the games of any other player—perhaps even more so than in those of Capablanca.

—Byrne

After 15. Q–R3

Larsen–Fischer, Denver 1971.

15. . . .	B–R3!

Black's strategy is to exchange a partially blocked Bishop for an unblocked one.

16. B–Q3	. . .

The KP must be further guarded but not by 16. P–B3 because of 16. . . . N–R4 followed by 17. . . . N–B5.

16. . . .	Q–B2
17. NPxP	NPxBP
18. PxP	PxP
19. B–B2	. . .

As early as the opening, a King's Indian Defense, White's plans focused on the Queenside and Black's on the other.

19. . . .	P–R3
20. N/2–K4	BxB

| 21. NxNch | RxN |
| 22. KRxB | QR–KB1 |

· The bloodletting has furthered Black's plans but done nothing for White's.

| 23. R–N6 | B–B1 |
| 24. N–K2? | . . . |

Relatively best is 24. P–B4, preventing Black's next move, but the strategic battle has already been decided.

| 24. . . . | P–B5! |

Threatening 24. . . . P–B6. Tactics take over from strategy.

| 25. B–K4 | N–B4 |
| 26. R–B6 | . . . |

Or 26. K–R1 R–R3 27. N–N1 Q–K2, followed by 28. . . . N–Q5 and 29. . . . Q–R5, with a huge attack.

26. . . .	Q–KN2!
27. R–N1	N–R5!
28. Q–Q3	. . .

If 28. RxB RxR 29. Q–R3 R/1–KB1 30. QxN R–R3! wins.

| 28. . . . | B–B4 |

Threatening both 29. . . . QxPch and 29. . . . NxP.

| 29. K–R1 | . . . |

If 29. P–N3 PxP 30. BPxP BxB 31. QxB N–B6ch wins.

29. . . .	P–B6!
30. N–N3	PxPch
31. K–N1	BxB
32. QxB	N–B6ch
33. KxP	N–Q7
Resigns	

Black wins the Exchange, the KBP, and presses the mating onslaught.

The first and most important thing a player must do is to set an attainable goal.

—Lombardy

After 15. B–KB1

Tolush–Botvinnik, Moscow 1945.

| 15. . . . | P–QN4! |

Black's goal, even at such an early point, is to win the Endgame with a Queenside Pawn advance.

16. Q–B3	QR–N1
17. KR–N1	Q–B2
18. B–B1!	P–R4
19. B–R3	R–N3!
20. Q–N3	Q–Q1

Intending 21. . . . . Q–R5.

| 21. B–Q6 | RxB |

All part of the plan. Once the White QB disappears, Black cannot be prevented from exploiting his Queenside Pawn superiority.

22. PxR	B–B3
23. P–R3	K–Q2
24. R–K1	Q–R5

Getting the Queens off makes Black's task easier.

25. Q–K5	Q–B3
26. Q–N3	R–R5!
27. R–K3	R–B5
28. B–K2	Q–R5
29. B–B3	P–N5!

Success.

| 30. QxQ | . . . |

The position is lost for White. If 30. Q–R2 Q–B3 wins a pawn. If 30. PxP PxP 31. R–N1 QxQ 32. PxQ RxP 33. RxNP KxP and the extra Black Pawns eventually win. And if 30. BxP! PxB 31. R–K7ch KxP 32. QxQ RxQ 33. PxP PxP 34. RxP P–N6 35. PxP PxP 36.RxP P–N7 37. RxPch K–B2 38. R–N1 RxQP wins.

30. . . .	RxQ
31. P–N3	R–R1!
32. PxP	PxP
33. R–N1	R–QN1
34. P–R4	R–N2!
35. K–R2	KxP
36. P–N4	N–B6
37. R–QR1	. . .

Or 37. RxN2 P–B3 followed by 38. . . . P–K4, and Black wins.

37. . . .	N–N4
38. R–Q1	R–R2
39. P–R5	P–N4
40. K–N2	R–R7

White sealed 41. B–K2 and then resigned.

The plan must be in keeping with the characteristics of the position.

—Steinitz

After 23. . . . N–B3

Reshevsky–Najdorf, Argentina 1953.

| 24. P–B6! | . . . |

Positionally and tactically "in keeping with the position," this move soon results in a passed QBP and also splits Black's Pawns.

| 24. . . . | PxP |
| 25. PxP | Q–K3 |

White garners a piece on 25. . . . QxP?? 26. N–Q5.

| 26. P–QR4 | Q–N6 |

Meaningful counterplay is not to be found. If 26. . . . N–N5 27. N–Q5 is quite strong.

27. P–N5	PxP
28. PxP	R–QN1
29. P–R3	. . .

Safety first. There is no hurry.

29. . . .	Q–N5
30. K–R2	R–KB1
31. Q–K2	. . .

The Queen is needed on the other side.

31. . . .	R–QR1

Likewise fatal is the Pawn grab 31. . . . NxP 32. N–Q5! Q–R4 33. B–N6! PxB 34. QxN QxP 35. P–B7 R–B1 36. N–K7.

32. P–N6	PxP

If 32. . . . NxP 33. N–Q5 Q–N6 34. NxP wins.

33. P–B7	. . .

White's strategy, the creation of a passed QBP, has worked perfectly, and the game has been decided.

33. . . .	R–QB1
34. Q–N5!	Q–R6

Or 34. . . . QxQ 35. NxQ N–K1 36. BxP (threatening 37. N–R7) and White wins a piece.

35. QxNP	. . .

Threatening 36. Q–N7.

35. . . .	Q–R1
36. N–N5	N–K1
37. Q–B6	Q–R7
38. Q–N7	Q–K3
39. N–R7	RxP
40. RxR	NxR
41. QxN	Resigns

Utilizing an attack in one sector of the board as a preparation for pressing a decision in another is one of the most impressive strategical devices.

After 17. . . . P–B4

Bogolyubov–Selesniev, Mahrisch-Ostrau 1923.

18. N–Q5! . . .

Very direct, very strong. An attack on the Queenside begins.

18. . . . **R–B2**

If 18. . . . BxN 19. QxBch K–R1 20. PxP NxP 21. QxNP and White wins. If 18. . . . Q–Q1 (19. N–K7ch loomed) 19. P–K5 PxP 20. PxP favors White.

19. P–B5! **QPxP**

If 19. . . . Q–K3 20. PxQP PxQP 21. PxP NxP 22. R–K1 Q–Q2 23. P–KN4 N–R5 24. R–K7! wins for White.

20. P–K5! . . .

The play is shifting rightward. Threat: 21. N–B6ch K–R1 22. BxB PxB 23. RxP with a winning position.

20. . . .	**BxN**
21. BxB	**N–K3**
22. R–KB2!!	**P–B3?**

Better is 22. . . . R–K2.

23. BxN	QxB
24. R–Q2	R–K1
25. RxP	R/2–K2
26. R–B4	Q–B1
27. R/4–Q4!	. . .

A steamroller.—Eckstrom.

| 27. . . . | Q–B2 |
| 28. P–KR4! | . . . |

With absolute control of the Queen-file, White now presses the decision on the Kingside.

| 28. . . . | K–N2 |

Or 28. . . . P–KR4 29. R–Q6 K–R2 30. R–B6! and White wins.

29. P–KN4!	PxP
30. QxP	K–R1
31. P–R5!	R–B2
32. PxP	PxP
33. R–Q7!	. . .

Avoiding loss of the Queen with 33. QxP?? R–R2ch 34. K–N1 R–N2.

33. . . .	Q–R4
34. QxP!	QxRch
35. RxQ	R–R2ch
36. QxRch	KxQ
37. K–N3	Resigns

The two connected passed Pawns make it easy.

The plan of play at a particular point in the game is called the strategical plan: the way in which it is laid out, the collection of principles we follow in its determination, is known as strategy.

—Pachman

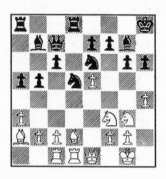

After 20. QR–B1

Panno–Evans, Haifa 1976.

20. . . .	P–QB4!

With an advantage on the light squares, pressure on the KP, and well-placed pieces, Black seizes the initiative. Threat: 21. . . . P–B5, seriously cramping White.

21. P–B4?!	PxP
22. KBxP	P–R5

The backward QNP is a greater liability than the isolated QRP and QBP.

23. N–K4	Q–N3
24. Q–K2	B–QB3
25. R–N1	Q–N2!

Threatening to win a clear Exchange with 26. . . . N/4–B5 27. QBxN NxB 28. Q–K3 BxN 29. QxN BxR 30. RxB P–K3.

26. N–B3	N–Q5!
27. KNxN	PxN

28. NxN	BxN
29. BxB	QxB

Strategic exchanges have created a dominating centralized position and an expanding QP.

30. P–B4	P–B3
31. R–K1	. . .

Also unsatisfactory is 31. PxP PxP followed by . . . P–B4, and Black obtains an additional hold on the center and the probable takeover of the King-file.

31. . . .	PxP
32. PxP	QR–B1
33. Q–Q3	R–B3
34. QR–B1	R–K3
35. R–B4	Q–N4
36. B–N4	P–R4

Preparing . . . K–R2 and the capture of the KP and leaving White helpless.

37. P–QN3?	PxP
38. QxQNP	RxP
39. R–Q1	R–K5
40. R–B5	Q–K7!
41. R–KN5	P–Q6!

All the Black pieces are menacing. Threat: 42. . . . B–Q5ch 43. K–R2 RxP mate.

42. B–K1	B–Q5ch
Resigns	

For if 43. K–R2 B–B7 44. BxB QxB 45. R–N3 RxPch 46. R–R3 Q–B5ch 47. K–R1 RxRch 48. PxR Q–B6ch 49. K–R2 Q–K7ch 50. K–R1 P–Q7 and the decisive threat is 51. . . . R–Q6.

Spot the weakness! Mobilize against it! Rack up the point!

After 13. Q–K2

Addison–Bisguier, New York 1962–63.

      13. . . .   Q–R1

Black's strategy is to exchange the light-square Bishops and then exploit the weakness of White's Pawn structure.

      14. P–B4   **PxP**
      15. BxB   . . .

On 15. PxP BxB 16. QxB QxQch 17. KxQ the hanging Pawns hurt.

      15. . . .   **QxB**
      16. PxP   **P–QN4!**

The winning move from a strategical viewpoint.

      17. P–B5   . . .

If 17. PxP R–B7! is too powerful.

      17. . . .   **NxP!**

A sacrifice-investment based on the Queen's control of the QR1–KR8 slant.

18. PxN	BxPch
19. R–B2	BxRch
20. QxB	R–B7

Threatening 21. . . . N–K5 as well as 21. . . . RxB.

| 21. Q–Q4 | Q–N3! |

Forcing a winning Endgame.

22. QxQ	PxQ
23. B–B1	R–Q1
24. N–B1	. . .

And not 24. N/K–B3?? N–K5! 25. NxN R–Q8 mate!

| 24. . . . | R–Q8 |
| 25. B–N2 | RxR |

White gets counterplay with 25. . . . RxNch 26. RxR RxB 27. R–B1.

| 26. BxR | RxQRP |

With a Rook and three Pawns for a Bishop and a Knight the remainder is not difficult.

27. B–Q4	N–Q4
28. N–B3	P–N5
29. N/1–Q2	K–B1
30. K–B1	R–B7
31. K–K1	P–B3
32. K–Q1	R–B1
33. K–K2	K–K2

And the end came with 34. K–Q3 K–Q2 35. N–B4 P–QN4 36. N–R5 N–B6 37. N–Q2 K–Q3 38. N–N7ch K–B3 39. N–B5 K–Q4 40. N–Q7 N–R5, White resigns. It would be only a matter of time before the Rook penetrated and the QNPs advanced.

It is no easy matter to reply to Lasker's bad moves.

—Anonymous

After 13. . . . B–N2

Kavalek–Zeshkovsky, Manila 1976.

14. P–K5?! . . .

A bad move? True, it breaks the pawn front, cedes Q5, opens the QR1–KR8 diagonal for Black's QB, and fixes the KP and QP as targets; but on the plus side the KP becomes a dangerous wedge in Black's position and the scope of the KB is increased.

14. . . .	**QR–Q1**
15. Q–N4	. . .

Playing for mate!

15. . . .	**N–B3**
16. KR–Q1	**P–K3**
17. P–KR4	**Q–Q2**
18. P–R5	**BPxP**
19. BPxP	**N–N5**

Not 19. . . . NxQP? 20. BxN QxB 21. BxP and White wins. With the text, Black seeks to swap White's attacking KB.

20. PxP	**RPxP**
21. Q–R4!	. . .

No time is lost in preserving the KB.

21. . . .		NxB
22. RxN		R–B1
23. R/1–Q1		. . .

No exchanges when the order of the day is "Attack!"

23. . . .		R–B7
24. B–Q2		Q–Q1?

It is no easy matter . . . But some restraint, like 24. . . . P–QR4, might have made it easier.

25. Q–N4		R–K1
26. B–N4		Q–B1
27. R–KR3		P–R4

If 27. . . . R–B8 28. Q–R4! (28. RxR QxRch 29. K–R2 Q–N7!) 28. . . . RxRch 29. K–R2 P–B4 30. Q–R7ch K–B2 31. QxPch K–N1 32. N–R5! and White soon mates.

28. B–Q6		R–B6
29. P–B3		R–Q1
30. B–K7		BxKP
31. Q–R4		Resigns

After 31. . . . BxPch 32. K–R1, White mates at KR7.

It is not one move, even a very sharp one, that must be sought, but rather a workable strategy.

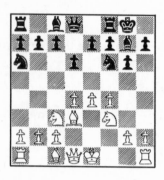

After 6. . . . N–R3

Mednis–Vadasz, Budapest 1976.

7. P–K5!	**. . .**

Defending his initiative. If 7. O–O P–B4 8. PxP NxBP and Black at least equalizes.

7. . . .	**N–Q2**
8. N–K4	**. . .**

The once-sharp move was the first shot in a battle for the Kingside.

8. . . .	**N–N5**

Black selects the wrong opening strategy—rapid piece development, which is generally the best! In this particular case, undermining the center—8. . . . P–QB4!—is correct.

9. B–K2	**N–N3**
10. P–B3	**B–B4**
11. N/3–N5	**P–Q4**
12. N–N3!	**. . .**

Rather than relinquish his Kingside plans, White sacrifices a Rook and gives up castling.

12. . . .	N–B7ch
13. K–B2	NxR
14. NxB	PxN
15. B–Q3	P–KR3

The winning line against 15. . . . P–K3 is 16. P–KN4! P–KR3 17. PxP! PxN 18. P–B6! BxP 19. Q–R5 R–K1 20. PxP! B–N2 21. K–K2! R–K2 22. R–B1 K–B1 23. P–N6 K–K1 24. B–N5 K–Q2 25. BxR PxP 26. QxP Q–R1 27. P–KR4 R–KN1 28. R–B7.

| 16. BxP! | P–K3 |

Against 16. . . . PxN, there follows 17. Q–R5 R–K1 18. P–K6 Q–Q3 19. B–R7ch K–R1 20. B–N6ch K–N1 21. BxPch K–B1 22. Q–R7 and White mates in three.

| 17. B–R7ch | K–R1 |
| 18. B–N1! | . . . |

Threatening 19. Q–Q3 and 20. Q–R7 mate.

| 18. . . . | P–KB4 |

Or 18. . . . Q–K2 19. Q–Q3 P–KB4 20. PxP e.p. BxP 21. NxP R–B2 22. R–K1, White would come out with a Bishop and two Pawns (the Knight on R8 is doomed) for a Rook and a continuing winning assault.

19. NxP	Q–K2
20. NxR	RxN
21. B–Q3	P–B4
22. B–K3	. . .

Two Pawns behind, Black is lost. It terminated with 22. . . . PxP 23. PxP N–B5 24. QxN NxB 25. KxN P–N4 26. Q–Q1 P–R3 27. P–KN3 Q–KB2 28. Q–B2 P–KR4 29. R–QB1 P–R5 30. Q–N2 PxP 31. PxP, Black resigns.

A difficult strategical problem is the decision to
play for the win of a pawn in the opening at the
expense of development.

—Pachman

After 11. QxN

Fuderer–Milic, Agram 1955.

      11. . . .   **Q–N4?**

Black neglects his development and goes Pawn hunting. With
11. . . . N–Q2 12. N–B3 PxP 13. BxP P–QN3 14. O–O B–N2 followed by . . . P–QB4, equal chances result.

        12. N–B3!   **QxP**
        13. K–K2   . . .

White's strategy is obvious—harass the Queen and mount an
attack on the KN-file. Threat: 14. P–KR3 and 15. QR–KN1 winning
the Queen.

        13. . . .   **Q–R6**
        14. QR–KN1   **P–KB4**
        15. R–N3   **Q–R4**
        16. KR–KN1   **R–B2**
        17. Q–R3!   . . .

Now the idea is 18. Q–Q6, 19. K–K1, and 20. N–K5, forcing the
Black Rook off the second rank.

17. . . .	N–Q2
18. K–K1	PxP
19. BxQBP	P–B5

With quantitative and qualitative inferiority in development, Black has no defense and is a sitting duck. Thus if 19. . . . N–N3 20. Q–Q6! NxB 21. Q–Q8ch K–R2 22. Q–K8! (threatening 23. RxPch!) P–KN4 23. RxP! PxR 24. RxP and White picks up everything.

| 20. RxPch | . . . |

Killing.

20. . . .	RxR
21. BxPch	K–R1
22. RxR	KxR
23. Q–K7ch	K–R1
24. N–K5!	PxP
25. P–B4	Resigns

Nothing can be done to counter the threat of 26. N–B7ch K–N2 27. N–N5ch K–N3 28. Q–B7 mate.

The judicious return of extra material is a mark of the master.

—Eckstrom

After 28. K–N1

Hernandez–Rogoff, Las Palmas 1976.

| 28. . . . | N/5xBP! |

Black returns his extra Knight in order to establish an Ending in which his Rook will dominate the board.

| 29. RxN | NxR |
| 30. KxN | K–Q4 |

Preventing 31. P–K4.

| 31. K–K2 | P–B4 |

To saddle White with an isolated KP.

32. PxP	KxP
33. N–B5	R–K3
34. K–B3	K–Q4
35. K–B4	. . .

If 35. K–N4 K–K5 wins.

35. . . .	R–K5ch
36. K–B3	P–KR4
37. K–B2	K–K3
38. N–N7ch	. . .

The combined pressure of the King and Rook is telling. The text loses material, but on the alternative 38. N–Q4ch K–B3 39. N–B3 R–KN5 40. P–KR3 R–N2 41. N–Q4 R–QB2 42. P–R4 R–B8 43. K–B3 K–K4 44. N–K2 R–KR8 45. K–N2 R–N8 46. N–Q4 K–K5 47. K–B2 R–N7ch 48. K–N3 KxP, Black also wins easily.

38. . . .	K–K4
39. NxP	RxRP
40. N–B4	RxPch
41. K–B3	RxP

Now, a clear Exchange to the good, it is only a matter of creating a passed Pawn to force resignation.

| 42. N–Q3ch | K–Q3 |
| 43. K–K4 | P–R4 |

44. K–Q4	P–N4
45. P–K4	R–QB7
46. N–B4	P–R5
47. PxP	PxP
48. P–K5ch	K–Q2
49. K–Q3	R–KR7
Resigns	

White must pay a Knight for the RP.

A Philosophy of Chess

Chess is many things to a few people and a few things to many people. A few millions play it, and billions have no idea what it is all about. To those who are enchanted by it, it is a game, a fight, a war in microcosm, an art, a science, an escape, an anodyne, a love affair, a way of life. And a myriad of other things. To those who are not bewitched by it, it is far less. A German proverb says, "No fool can play chess, and only fools do." George Bernard Shaw cracked, "Chess is a foolish expedient for making idle people believe they are doing something very clever, when they are only wasting their time." H. G. Wells opined: "It is a curse upon a man. There is no happiness in chess." Michel de Montaigne exclaimed, "I hate and avoid this idle, childish game." And Albert Einstein theorized, "Master chess grips its exponent, shackling the mind and brain so that the inner freedom and independence of even the strongest character cannot remain unaffected."

But the detractors are met head on. An Indian proverb says, "Chess is a sea in which a gnat may drink and an elephant may bathe." According to Thomas Huxley: "The chessboard is the world, the pieces are the phenomena of the universe, the rules of the game are what we call the laws of Nature. The Player on the other side is hidden from us. We know that his play is always fair, just, and patient. But we also know, to our cost, that he never overlooks a mistake, or makes the smallest allowance for ignorance." Dr. Siegbert Tarrasch wrote: "I have always a slight feeling of pity for the man who has no knowledge of chess, just as I would pity the man who has remained ignorant of love. Chess, like love, like music, has the power to make man happy." Aristotle advised, "When you are lonely, when you feel yourself an alien in the world, play chess. This will raise your spirits and be your counselor in war." Confucius said: "I greatly admire a fellow who goes about the whole day with a well-fed stomach and a vacuous mind. How can one ever do it? I would rather that he play chess, which would seem to me to be better." From Gottfried Leibnitz: "I strongly commend the practice of chess and other games of reason, not for themselves, but because they help perfect the art of thinking." And Benjamin Franklin observed: "The Game of Chess is not merely an idle amusement; several very valuable qualities of the mind, useful in the course of human life, are to be acquired and strengthened by it, so as to become habits ready on all occasions; for life is a kind of Chess, in which we have points to gain, and competitors or adversaries to contend with, and in which there is a vast variety of good and ill events, that are, in some degree, the effect of prudence, or the want of it. By playing at Chess then, we may learn: Foresight, Circumspection, Caution, and Courage."

What is chess, then, that it elicits such divergent opinions from authors, philosophers, scientists, and physicians? Why is it a waste of time to some and a help in perfecting the art of thinking to others? Surely, the answer is not wholly in Funk & Wagnalls's definition: "A game of skill played on a chessboard by two persons, with 16 pieces on each side. The aim of each player, proceeding by alternate moves, is to checkmate his opponent's king." Nor is it in the staggering mathematical fact that the number of possible ways of playing the first ten moves on each side in a game is 169,-518,829,100,544,000,000,000,000,000. The answer may be something extremely difficult to verbalize. It may be that the pieces—the King, Queen, Rook, Bishop, Knight, and Pawn—with their varied geometric movements, somehow and to some degree duplicate the mysterious components of the human brain. And that these components, or geometric movements, supply the symbols for the thought processes. Then, with the processes operative, learning begins, memories are stored. Finally, thinking—"the manipulation of memories," according to Rudolf Flesch—is possible. Possessed of the components, the processes, and the memories, the mind of the chess player proceeds to call on the elements of vision (intuition of possibilities by the mind's eye), common sense, ideas, imagination, judgment, and memory to play his game. Tension, emotion, the excitement of carrying out a purpose under opposition, the creation of beauty, and the search for truth—the fascination of chess—all follow. A fascination which prompted Frank J. Marshall, U.S. Champion 1909–36, to exult: "My entire life has been devoted to the game. I don't believe a day has gone by that I have not played at least one game of chess—and I still enjoy it as much as ever."

Anybody can learn to play chess; nobody can master it. Marshall wrote: "You can learn the moves in fifteen minutes. In another fifteen minutes you can get the idea of the game, and you can play within the hour." But Tarrasch noted, "Many have become chess masters—no one has become the master of chess." To become proficient at the game, much is required. One must be genetically endowed with native talent, one must have a passion for it, must be devoted to it. One must learn it at an early age, have a good teacher, and spend years of study on it. One must be a member of a club, a state association, and the national Federation. And one must play for fun and for blood, play speed chess and tournament chess, climb the ladder of success up through the classes, to Expert, Master, Senior Master, International Master, and finally to Grand-master, by competing in organized tournaments sponsored by the United States Chess Federation and the International Federation of Chess.

Most chess players are also chess-book readers, enjoying study almost as much as play. And there are plenty for them to read, more books having been written on chess than on all other games combined. "The intelligent perusal of fine games," wrote Lasker, "cannot fail to make the reader a better player and a better judge of the play of others"; but he insisted that all notes be read critically. Nonsense in chess books, as in others, is, unfortunately, not too scarce.

How and what to study is of great significance. James Mason observed "that due knowledge of any subject not perfectly simple in itself implies exact knowledge of its elements or parts is a truism remarkably appropriate to chess." And chess, like ancient Gaul, is divided into three parts—three parts which are best studied in reverse order: endgame, middlegame and opening. The Endgame first, especially Rook-and-Pawn Endgames, because "a player in a fog as to the movements of two or three pieces—what will he do with two-and-thirty?" Each of the pieces, major, minor, and Pawns, and their various groupings must also be studied to appreciate their particular powers and peculiarities, powers which are the basis of all combinations. For a really good player must be an all-around player, one at home in any part of the game, fully able to handle all the pieces and play imaginatively and combinatively, and one versed in the strategical subtleties of positional play or the give-and-take melee of tactical play. Rudolf Spielmann summed it up: **"In the Opening a master should play like a book, in the Mid-game he should play like a magician, in the Ending he should play like a machine."**

Chess, or chaturanga, a game substantially like chess, was born in Mother India about A.D. 500. Developing and changing as it went along, it traveled from India to Persia to Arabia. Then, around A.D. 1300 the Moors took it to Spain, thence it spread across Europe, and finally the early settlers brought it to America. In Colonial days, it was a pastime of only the affluent and intelligentsia. At least three of the Founding Fathers—Washington, Jefferson, and Franklin—played. But it was not until the advent of Paul Morphy, 1837–84, that the game achieved any real popularity. Since that Civil War period, the scene has been successively dominated by William Steinitz, Emanuel Lasker, Harry Nelson Pillsbury, Frank James Marshall, José Raoul Capablanca, and Samuel Reshevsky. And now it is the Age of Robert James Fischer.

The Fischer Boom, the time during which chess reached its greatest popularity in the United States, began in 1957/58 when he won the U.S. Championship at the age of fourteen, continued while he won the next seven U.S. Championships in a row, and reached its height when he defeated Boris Spassky of the U.S.S.R. to win the World Championship at Reykjavik in 1972. Now the boom is over.

What causes a boom? What is needed to make the game grow and prosper? Steinitz insisted chess must be self-supporting. According to Lasker, "The future belongs to the creative master and to an organization which works in unison with him." And today the conventional wisdom is that the game must be promoted in local clubs, in state associations, in weekend Swiss tournaments, and that it must be financed by foundations.

Chess is not generally recognized as a spectator sport. There is no chance that Yankee Stadium will ever be filled to watch Fischer play Karpov at a chess table located near second base. Lasker is more realistic. The conventional wisdom is not wholly wise because the pool of chess players from which the clubs, associations, and the federation can draw is too small; players make tournaments, not the other way around, and the existing foundations are unable to fund all that is necessary.

More people must be brought into chess, hundreds of thousands, millions of people. The general public must be educated to appreciate it. There must be more women in chess, as there are in bridge and backgammon. Only 1 percent of the members of the U.S. Chess Federation are female—making the chess society virtually a monastic order. More children must be taught the game in schools, in camps, in the Girl Scouts, and in the Boy Scouts. Children take to the game very readily and learn it more easily than most adults. Grandmaster tours and Grandmaster matches must be held on a regular schedule in order to produce creative, great games. Funding must be provided by the government, as it is in countries where the game flourishes; by corporations, as it has been here in a few instances and is done in some foreign lands; by existing and future foundations; and by private individuals. Relying on membership dues and sales profits, as the U.S.C.F. is forced to do, is a hopeless proposition. A nationwide publicity campaign is needed, on television and radio and in newspapers and magazines, to bring the history, lore, celebrities, competitiveness, fun, excitement, and mind-training qualities of the game to the country. And, perhaps above all else, the chess world should strive to bring back Fischer. For chess, like boxing with Muhammad Ali, needs a charismatic champion, a world beater, a hero to capture the media, a Morphy or a Bobby Fischer, to find its place in the sun.

But even with imperfect organization, inadequate financing,

inverse priorities, comparatively few players, poor promotion, scant publicity, and lack of a great star, the Royal Game will go on developing as it has for the last fifteen hundred years. Henry Bird, the famous English player, expressed it well when he wrote: "Chess is so ancient that, by that distinction alone, it seems beyond the category of games altogether; and it has been said that it probably would have perished long ago if it had not been destined to live forever."

Index of Players

Index of Games

Index of Openings

Index of Subjects

276 *Index of Subjects*

Opening

See also Index of Openings

Pawn(s)

Queened by force, 91–92

Queenside attack in Middlegame, 213–14

Queen

Pawn promotion in Queen and Pawn ending, 29–30

Rook(s)

Pawn grabbing at expense of development, 258–59